STUCK, UNSTUCK, UNSTOPPABLE,

High-Achieving Women - Discover, and Overcome the Obstacles to an Unstoppable You

JULI MIEZEJESKI

© 2025 ALL RIGHTS RESERVED.

Published by She Rises Studios Publishing **www.SheRisesStudios.com**.

No part of this book may be reproduced or transmitted in any form whatsoever, electronic, or mechanical, including photocopying, recording, or by any informational storage or retrieval system without the expressed written, dated and signed permission from the publisher and author.

LIMITS OF LIABILITY/DISCLAIMER OF WARRANTY:

The author and publisher of this book have used their best efforts in preparing this material. While every attempt has been made to verify the information provided in this book, neither the author nor the publisher assumes any responsibility for any errors, omissions, or inaccuracies.

The author and publisher make no representation or warranties with respect to the accuracy, applicability, or completeness of the contents of this book. They disclaim any warranties (expressed or implied), merchantability, or for any purpose. The author and publisher shall in no event be held liable for any loss or other damages, including but not limited to special, incidental, consequential, or other damages.

ISBN: 978-1-969463-43-3

DISCLAIMER

Some of the mental fitness tools and techniques in this book are like those used in psychotherapy. This book aims to support and guide you on your journey to mental fitness, personal growth, and living authentically. It is not a substitute for seeking professional help from licensed mental health professionals.

While I am a Certified Professional Coach trained through the Institute for Professional Excellence in Coaching (iPEC) and a Positive Intelligence Coach, I am not a licensed therapist, psychologist, or psychiatrist. The coaching methodologies, personal stories, and practical exercises in this book are based on my training and experience as a transformational life coach, but they should not be construed as therapy or medical advice.

If you are experiencing mental health challenges, trauma, or conditions that require clinical intervention, please seek the appropriate professional support.

The journey to mental fitness and authentic living is deeply personal. Use this book as a companion and guide, but always honor your own wisdom about when additional professional support would serve you best.

Table of Contents

Preface: My WHYs for Writing This Book 7

Introduction 9

Part One: The Brain's Development and Changes, Your Inner Child, and Intuition 13

Chapter One: How Your Brain Develops in Childhood: The Foundation of Your Inner Child 14

Chapter Two: How Your Inner Child Shows Up in Adult Life (Getting Stuck) 31

Chapter Three: The Journey of the Inner Child: From Loss to Rediscovery (Getting Unstuck) 46

Chapter Four: The Relationship of Your Inner Child To Your Intuition 53

Chapter Five: The Unconscious Mind – Your Hidden Brilliance .. 62

Part Two: Positive Intelligence (Mental Fitness) 69

Chapter Six: Introduction To Mental Fitness 70

Chapter Seven: Sabotaging Behaviors 74

Chapter Eight: Diane's Story – A Case Study 97

Chapter Nine: Sage Powers – Turning Every Challenge Into a Gift 104

Chapter Ten: Transformation, Reflection, and Growth Work for All Saboteurs 115

Part Three: The Unstoppable You 131

Chapter Eleven: Pathway To Purpose 132

Chapter Twelve: Breaking Free from Procrastination – When Your Avoider Saboteur Takes Control..137

Chapter Thirteen: The Daily Practice of Mindfulness – Strengthening Your Mental Fitness Muscle.......................146

Conclusion: Manifesting The Life You Choose 159

Acknowledgements...171

About the Author 173

Life Coaching With Juli..175

Bibliography 179

Preface

MY WHYS FOR WRITING THIS BOOK

Reluctance is the word I would use to describe my feelings about writing this section for this book. Up until I put my pen to paper, and yes, I still do sometimes write with pen and paper, I hesitated on not writing this part.

The fears I had during my corporate days, though almost 25 years ago, still crop up occasionally, subconsciously, making me pause before I act.

I first realized that my fears were totally unfounded about 15 years ago when I received my certification as a professional coach. However, it has taken me 15 years to feel strong enough within myself and love myself enough to heal beyond this realization.

Writing during my corporate career was all about business and nothing else, so there was no reason to write a section about why you were writing. It was all about facts and figures, analysis, and esoteric opinion.

My #1 WHY

This book is my first non-fiction, non-business book, and a true story about my journey and the journeys of other colleagues and clients from living as children, only using our intuition, to ego-based living as adolescents and young adults, to rediscovering and reconnecting to our intuition later in adulthood. Now we all depend on our gut, our intuition, more than ego-based logic to make decisions. As a result, we are all living happier and more fulfilling lives.

My #2 WHY

I wanted to prove to people who still live in the ego mind and ostracize others who believe in and live a more spiritual life, that intuition is proven by neuroscience. Still, I know there are groups of people who neither believe in intuition, spirituality, nor science, but that is their problem, not mine.

My #3 WHY

Realizing that I wasn't being the person I wanted to be for so many years of my life, it was time to 'come out' and show my authentic self. I am no longer afraid of being seen as an empath and have cracked the protective shield that my fears put around me.

My #4 and most important WHY

My mission is to encourage all women, especially those who are the younger version of my high-achieving self, to choose self-growth and authenticity over the status quo. All women deserve to be seen, heard, and empowered for the amazing women they are!

Introduction

Many years ago, I sat in my office overlooking New York City, surrounded by every symbol of success I had ever wanted. My husband and I had just built a beautiful four-bedroom colonial in northwestern New Jersey. My life appeared to be the pinnacle of success, but I felt empty.

This emptiness set me on a journey that changed everything. It took several years to understand what was causing these feelings. It was five years from that moment before I even began to grasp what was missing in my life.

Just before the turn of the century, a sudden insight shifted the direction of my life. Within just 15 minutes, my life's course changed, though I didn't realize it until the seeds planted during those minutes blossomed into a field of new opportunities in the emerging life coaching industry.

Instead of remaining a small part of a corporate machine, I started the journey to reconnect with my authentic self—my inner child, my creativity, my empathy, and my deep desire to help others. This longing to serve others originated in childhood, was forgotten as I grew into adulthood, and reemerged when I decided to become a life coach.

The importance of our intuition has been largely ignored by society in general. But for thousands of years, people relied solely on intuition. In recent years, intuitives like myself have been "coming out of the closet," no longer fearing what others might say. Many still dismiss us as believing in "woo-woo."

As infants, our spirits are untouched. During the first five to seven years, we live in imaginary worlds—worlds guided by pure intuition. We are born with a spiritual purpose and lessons to learn. As children, our imagination guides us to be who we want to be—for ourselves and others.

Yet, when influenced by adults who live entirely in the ego world, we gradually lose our inner child, our imagination, and our innate creativity, and forget our authentic selves.

I'm not generalizing; this doesn't happen to everyone. In fact, those who retain their inner child and grow into who they truly want to be are the lucky ones. Many of the most successful people in the world never lose their intuition; their inner child remains with them throughout life.

For those of us whose inner child becomes wounded or forgotten, we may develop self-saboteurs like the judge, the controller, the hyper-achiever, the stickler, the avoider, the hyper-rational, the victim, the hyper-vigilant, the restless, and the pleaser.

All of these archetypes are detailed in this book. They are behavioral patterns that prevent us from facing life's challenges with a positive mindset. Instead, we often become upset and stressed.

The book also explores five "sage powers": empathy, exploration, innovation, navigation, and activation—all explained in more detail later in this book.

These ideas are further elaborated in Positive Intelligence by Shirzad Chamine.

Mainly, this book reflects my journey to rediscover my inner child and to make sense of it all. I wrote it to help others who are on similar paths or have been there.

With heartfelt love, I hope high-achieving women—especially those who are younger versions of myself—will find this book beneficial. Maybe, instead of struggling for years to find answers, they will be guided toward their authentic selves earlier in life.

My wish is that everyone who reads this book will experience a life filled with fulfillment and happiness.

PART ONE

The Brain's Development and Changes, Your Inner Child, and Intuition

Chapter One

How Your Brain Develops in Childhood: The Foundation of Your Inner Child

The first seven to eight years of a child's life are incredibly important for brain development. Think of this period as building the foundation of a house—everything that comes later depends on how strong and stable that foundation is. While our brains keep growing and changing throughout our lives, these early years create the basic structure that shapes how we think, feel, and relate to others for the rest of our lives.

Three main factors influence how a child's brain develops: genetics (what they inherit from their parents), proper nutrition, and, most importantly for understanding the inner child, their experiences with the people around them.

The inner child. We all have one hidden somewhere inside us, don't we? That magical part of ourselves that once saw the world through eyes of wonder before life's realities dimmed their sparkle.

When we enter the world, our inner child begins taking shape - a wild, untamed creature bounding through fields of possibility. During these early years, our brains are buzzing with activity, forming neural connections at mind-boggling rates - about a million per second in those first precious years. The prefrontal cortex, amygdala, and hippocampus work overtime, creating emotional patterns that stick with us like shadows that never quite disappear, even on the darkest nights.

Kids naturally embody what we call the inner child - that spontaneous, playful spirit that jumps in puddles without worrying about muddy shoes. Their right-brain dominance lets them play make-believe without questioning whether unicorns are "logical" or not. This is our authentic inner child in its purest form, prancing freely across open fields.

Here's what's remarkable: every experience a child has changes their brain. Positive experiences—like being comforted when upset, feeling safe and loved, or having consistent, caring responses from parents—build certain pathways in the brain. Negative experiences—like being ignored, criticized harshly, or experiencing unpredictable care—build different pathways. Over time, these experiences add up to create lasting patterns in how we respond emotionally and behaviorally. These patterns become like invisible templates that guide how we handle relationships, process our emotions, and make sense of the world as adults.

During the first three years of life, something amazing happens in a child's brain. It grows faster than it ever will again, creating connections at an incredible rate. By age three, a child has about 1,000 trillion brain connections—more than they'll ever have in their entire life.

But here's the fascinating part: the brain doesn't keep all these connections. It follows a "use it or lose it" rule. The connections that get used repeatedly become stronger and permanent. The ones that don't get used often enough get eliminated or "pruned away." This process is like a sculptor chiseling away excess stone to reveal the final statue—the brain sculpts itself based on the child's experiences.

This sculpting process directly creates what we call the inner child. When a child repeatedly experiences safety, love, and consistent care, their brain strengthens the pathways connected to trust, emotional balance, and feeling secure in relationships. But when a child experiences neglect, inconsistency, or harm, their brain may eliminate connections related to feeling safe and trusting others, while strengthening pathways related to being constantly on guard, having difficulty managing emotions, or protecting themselves through various defensive behaviors.

The relationships a child has with their parents and caregivers directly shape how their brain develops. When adults consistently respond to a baby's cries with comfort and care, they're helping to build strong brain pathways that connect emotional upset with the expectation of help and relief. This creates what becomes the foundation of a secure inner child—a deep, internal sense of being safe and worthy of love.

This secure foundation doesn't just affect emotions; it impacts a child's willingness to explore and learn. Children who feel secure in their relationships develop stronger brain connections that support curiosity, the ability to take healthy risks, and resilience when facing challenges. Neurologically speaking, this becomes the inner child's natural capacity for wonder, creativity, and authentic self-expression.

As we navigate middle childhood (ages 6-11), our brains continue developing, allowing for more complex social connections. We start figuring out how we fit in with others, though we still hold onto much of that playful spirit, building forts from couch cushions and seeing magical kingdoms in backyard trees.

Think of it this way: when a child knows they have a safe base to return to, they feel free to venture out and discover the world. This sense of security gets wired into their brain and becomes part of how they approach life as an adult.

Then comes adolescence, bringing significant shifts in our brain's architecture. Neural pathways get pruned like overgrown branches, eliminating less-used connections while strengthening others. Our prefrontal cortex continues developing, improving our ability to think rationally and control impulses, but sometimes at the cost of that beautiful spontaneity. Suddenly, what friends think becomes all-important, creating the first serious threat to our authentic self-expression.

This biological process explains why the emotional and relationship patterns we learned in early childhood can feel so automatic and hard to change as adults. The brain pathways formed during those critical early years become like superhighways—information travels along them quickly and without much conscious thought.

Understanding this helps explain why certain inner child responses can feel so immediate and out of our control. These aren't character flaws or weaknesses; they're highly efficient brain patterns that were created during childhood and became permanent features of how our brains operate.

Different Stages of Childhood Brain Development

Children's brains are most flexible and changeable during different periods, and each stage affects inner child development in unique ways:

Ages 0-3: Maximum Brain Flexibility. During these early years, the brain can adapt and change more easily than at any other time in life. This is when a child's core sense of safety, worth, and basic trust gets established through thousands of small interactions with their parents and caregivers. Every time a parent responds to a crying baby, plays peek-a-boo, or provides comfort, they're helping to wire the child's brain for security and connection.

Ages 3-7: The Creative Years. This is when children develop the ability to use symbols, engage in imaginative play, and express themselves creatively. During this phase, the brain supports the inner child's natural capacity for wonder, creativity, and magical thinking. Children this age don't think in terms of strict rules yet, which allows for maximum creative and emotional expression. They can believe in fairy tales, have imaginary friends, and see possibilities everywhere.

Ages 7-11: Learning Rules and Fairness. As thinking skills develop, children understand rules, fairness, and social expectations. They start caring about winning games and understanding justice. This developmental shift can either support healthy inner child development or contribute to suppressing it, depending on how the adults around them respond to their natural creativity and emotional expressions.

By the time children reach their teenage years, the number of brain pathways begins to stabilize, and the brain focuses on strengthening the connections that are used most often while continuing to prune away those that aren't needed.

The key insight is this: your brain developed in childhood exactly as it needed to help you survive your particular circumstances. The patterns that may cause problems in your adult relationships were once protective strategies for your young brain.

The development of brain pathways in early childhood provides both the explanation for how your inner child was formed and the roadmap for healing and integrating it in your adult life. The same brain flexibility that created these patterns in childhood can be accessed in adulthood to create new, more supportive ways of thinking, feeling, and relating to others.

Case Studies

Lisa's Story

Lisa's earliest memory is lying in her crib wearing blue corduroy slippers with animals, looking out a window. She remembers feeling profound sadness and a sense of waiting, wondering if her father had just walked out and left her mother crying. This memory corresponds to when her father committed suicide when she was six months old, making this her first experience of loss.

Neurodevelopmental research shows that Lisa's first memory, "even in preverbal children, encodes the emotional climate of trauma in the amygdala and right hemisphere, priming lifelong patterns of vigilance, sadness, or existential 'waiting.'…loss or disruption of a primary caregiver in infancy often results in anxious or disorganized attachment, deeply impacting self-worth and relationships later in life."

Living with her grandmother after her father's death, Lisa felt uneasy about her mother's impending remarriage. Even at three, she sensed everything would change again and didn't like her future stepfather. When her grandmother encouraged her to "be a big girl" about the situation, Lisa's internal response was "I'm already a big girl and I still don't like it."

Her grandmother's response to "be a big girl" is an example of "parentification or adultification, in which children are forced to suppress feelings and are forced to perform mature roles too early."

In her new home with her stepfather, Lisa had a recurring nightmare about being chased up a spiral staircase by a threatening man. When she called out for comfort, her stepfather coldly responded, "Just put the covers over your head," reinforcing her negative feelings about him and demonstrating his lack of care.

Lisa's experience in this instance represents "psychological wounding caused by lack of emotional validation."

When given half a grapefruit with instructions not to add sugar, Lisa mistakenly put salt on it instead. Rather than understanding it was an innocent mistake, her parents made her eat the salted grapefruit as punishment for "not listening." This experience crystallized her sense of unworthiness at just five years old.

When her sister was born (Lisa was 4), she experienced intense jealousy over her sister's beauty and the attention she received. In a moment of childhood desperation, Lisa cut off her sister's eyelashes, then felt guilty about also cutting her doll's eyelashes because "they would never grow back, but my sister's lashes would"—showing an intuitive understanding even as a small child.

This birth marked Lisa's transition from being the precious first grandchild to becoming "the person that helps with everything," losing her special status in the family. My research further shows that "traumatized children can internalize guilt and further displace their needs to maintain harmony in the family."

As a child, Lisa loved drawing, crafts, string games like Jacob's Ladder, creating miniature worlds with Lincoln Logs and Matchbox cars, and exploring nature. She was particularly drawn to rocks and minerals, spending entire afternoons cracking open stones to discover what was inside—a metaphor for her lifelong curiosity about hidden depths.

Starting at age 10, Lisa learned drums and organ, showing natural musical ability that continues today with drums, ukulele, and guitar.

Lisa carries the burdens of previous generations of women who "endured atrocities and lived through a lot," inheriting "that heaviness and that sense of false level of responsibility." She didn't understand this generational trauma until her sixties.

Her aunts, grandmother, and great-grandmother provided the nurturing and encouragement missing from her immediate family. These women were "more educated, interesting, and had more patience and desire to foster what was great about me." Her Aunt (with nine children) was very creative and resourceful, while her other aunt was an artist. These women served as her true role models, and she remains close to her cousins from these relationships.

Between the ages of 10-13, during a period of household unrest, Lisa experienced sexual abuse from her stepfather. When she finally told her mother at 14, her mother's response was constrained by fear and financial dependence—she couldn't leave because "where are we going?" This forced all family members to continue suffering because of their mother's fears. The sexual abuse by her stepfather and her mother's inability to protect her reinforce deep patterns of betrayal trauma, helplessness, and silencing of the inner child.

The abuse coincided with broader harassment from neighborhood boys and adult men, creating a pattern where Lisa felt "hunted" and "objectified" as soon as she developed physically, transitioning "from tomboy to boobs."

During her lonely teenage years (12-14), Lisa created an imaginary boyfriend, using a picture from a wallet she received as a gift. She carried the wallet to school and told classmates about her "boyfriend," demonstrating her need for connection and her developing imagination as a coping mechanism.

***

Jane's Story

During my research for this book, I met a colleague who was willing to share her story of transformation, becoming unstuck from her early childhood lack of confidence in herself and other associated behaviors, to personal growth and self-awareness.

Jane's (name changed for anonymity) earliest memories date back to around age two. The interview follows in her words, "being launched into the air by my dad in something we called a 'rocket ship', and playing downstairs in our family home with my siblings. I shared a room with both my brother and sister when I was younger.

I always felt I was the odd one out in the family. As the youngest, I was generationally different from my solid boomer siblings— I grew up during cultural shifts, so changes that seemed dramatic to my family were simply the way things were for me. This made me naturally progressive and gave me a different worldview, which persists today as I live in another country from my family.

My brother was often sick throughout childhood—he had nearly every childhood illness except chicken pox, required allergy shots three times a week, and had to travel to New York City for treatment for another condition. This obviously weighed on my parents in both time and energy.

Coming along five years later as a healthy child, I felt an unspoken expectation to 'keep everybody happy' and 'keep things light.' While my parents did their best to maintain normalcy, child me internalized the perceived pressure to be the easy one who didn't require additional attention or resources."

As the youngest with a chronically ill sibling, Jane internalized the role of "the easy one," a classic adaptation when parental attention and resources are occupied. Academically, this adaptive role—known as "parentification" or "good child syndrome"—stems from unspoken family needs and often results in chronic self-suppression, making the child's wants secondary to maintaining family harmony.

* * *

My Story

I was born on a wintry night in January of 1955 by emergency C-section. The reason for my nonconventional entry into the world was that the umbilical cord broke between my mother and me. Time was of the essence, and my father had to get my mom and me to the hospital ASAP. I was drowning inside my mother's womb. And my mother was hemorrhaging.

When they got to the hospital, there happened to be workers outside working on the power lines. Someone from the hospital had to go out and tell them not to, under any circumstances, shut the power off. An emergency surgery was in progress.

Now I don't know if the hospital that I was born in had an emergency generator or not, but regardless of the fact, that's what the story was. It was touch-and-go for a few days; my Mom and Dad didn't know if I would live or not. That was the beginning of my life.

I often wondered if my birth experience had any effect on my brain development. I wondered if any neural pathways were damaged in the process, and my little brain had to work so hard to repair them in those first few days.

Our brains begin developing in the womb. By birth, our brains are a quarter of the size of an adult brain. The brain doubles in size in the first year. It keeps growing to about 80% of adult size by age 3 and 90% – nearly fully grown – by age 5.

A baby's brain is hard at work, forming over 1 million new neural connections per second. These connections enable everything from movement to language and problem-solving. They don't form on their own; positive interactions with caregivers and engaging daily experiences help build and strengthen these pathways that can last a lifetime if the same interactions and later life experiences strengthen them.

During my research for this story, I found that, indeed, "perinatal trauma and medical crises during infancy can profoundly impact the formation of neural pathways associated with stress response, emotional regulation, and later attachment behaviors. The newborn brain is highly plastic but also sensitive, predisposing individuals to heightened stress reactivity and influencing later patterns of resilience or vulnerability."

My first memory was sitting in a high chair in our family kitchen, looking at something through the kitchen window. My mother was ironing clothes and talking to me. I sense that she may have been pointing out a bird sitting on a tree branch, as I remember she often did.

I remember as a toddler, my mother taught me about all the bugs, the flowers, trees, small animals like squirrels, we had a lot of squirrels, and tall trees where I lived. She taught me the alphabet and counting numbers before I went to kindergarten. I know this only because I remember saying the alphabet and counting to ten on the first day of kindergarten. After all, my mother told me to do that for the teacher. That first day of kindergarten was my second major memory.

My mother went back to work as soon as she could after I started kindergarten. She graduated from Katherine Gibbs Secretarial School in Manhattan and held a job as an executive secretary before she gave birth to my brothers and stayed home as a housewife for almost fifteen years.

She couldn't wait to go back to work because she thrived when she had a sense of autonomy. She instilled this quality in me throughout my life, and she became my role model.

My next memory (also in kindergarten) was of a spanking that Sister Pancratia gave me in front of the whole classroom because, instead of waiting for her instructions, I began to draw with crayons on a piece of paper that was not meant to be drawn on. This was the first and only spanking I received in my life, so obviously it was very traumatic. This happened before the lunch period, and I remember crying so hard I couldn't eat my lunch. Those nuns had a lot of pent-up anger and frustration, and we little children, suffered the brunt of it.

This first trauma, receiving public punishment from an authority figure, according to my research, caused "acute humiliation and emotional pain." As a result, my inner child was wounded and "shaping future neural pathways to avoid visibility or risk and contributing to emotional dysregulation. The event demonstrates how toxic authority figures can incite protective, learned behaviors, such as appeasement or withdrawal, in an attempt to regain safety or acceptance."

My after-school caregiver was my maternal grandmother, and I loved her dearly. She treated me like a little princess. She was so sweet and loving, had no expectations of me, and like they used to say back in those days, she 'spoiled me rotten'. I could never be spoiled rotten (so to speak) because I was just too good a little girl. I was. Even though I didn't know it then, I have always been a hyper-sensitive person and felt, not only my hurts, but those of other people very strongly. After school, she used to give me her spare change and send me down to the candy store and let me pick out whatever I wanted. I still had all my baby teeth at first, so technically it didn't matter, but in subsequent years, my grandmother was probably to blame for my mouth full of cavities.

When I started third or fourth grade, I can't remember exactly, I became a latch-key kid, meaning I went home after school instead of to my grandmother's, and I was home at first, only about an hour or two alone before my brothers came home from school. I remember the routine of calling my Mom at work to report in that I was safe and sound, and then I watched TV until my Dad came home first, and sat and talked to him for a little while before he went to pick my Mom up at the train station. I loved that time because not only was it my first experience of being alone in the house, but it was my alone time with my Dad when he came home from work. After dinner, everyone went to do their own thing. My Mom did house chores, my brothers and I did our homework, and my Dad watched TV.

My mother was an executive secretary and made a better salary than most women in those days, and my Dad was a supervisor of welders in the Brooklyn Navy Yard. Although my father was considered a blue-collar worker, he was smart and was able to advance to a supervisor level, where he no longer had to do the hard work of his 200 subordinates and made a good salary as well. Thus, my brothers and I all went to private schools, which provided better education at the time than the New York City public school system. My parents were able to provide us with all that we ever wanted monetarily. So, they did so and saved money as well.

We always took summer family vacations, which were road trips to destinations between Niagara Falls and the south. I remember some of the trips, especially the one to Niagara Falls, probably because I was old enough at that time to appreciate the significance of it. I have a traumatic memory of one of the trips to the south when I was three, because my brothers and I took a walk in the woods of a campground while my parents were grilling food for dinner. My brothers left me by a small waterfall while they used small stones to cross a creek. They told me to wait there, and of course, when I lost sight of them, I started crying. My father came along looking for us and saw me by myself just before they returned, and boy, did they get in trouble! Luckily, though, being Boy Scouts, my brothers were smart enough to mark the trees along our way so we wouldn't get lost, and my Dad found us with no problem.

Although we had rich experiences as children and wanted for nothing monetarily as children, my siblings and I faced a sometimes tense and scary atmosphere in our household. My father was a manic depressive (called bipolar today), and it was often difficult to predict what his mood would be like every day. In those days, there were no mood-regulating medications, not even lithium yet, I don't think. He had shock treatments at one point, but I don't remember that. It might have been before I was born. As a result, we would tiptoe around the house, never knowing what to expect. He was physically abusive to my brothers at times, but physically abusive only once to me when he slapped me because I accidentally broke a set of rosary beads. He would yell at me a lot, oftentimes I didn't even know why, and being as sensitive as I was, I would run into my room crying and stay there for hours. My inner child saved me during these times, as I was able to escape and temporarily forget what happened. I would escape to my little world where I could be happy.

I never remember being praised for good work in school or exercising any kind of especially good behavior, as I often saw my friends' parents give them praise. They also received hugs from their parents, and I never received hugs from mine. I remember my Mom giving me what seemed like obligatory kisses on the cheek when she tucked me in at night and when she left me for the day in the morning. I don't remember any true affection, and I suffered from that. My parents, especially my Dad, just seemed to expect good behavior and good grades. I think my sabotaging people-pleasing behavior stems from my childhood because of this expectation put upon me as a child.

I felt this constant need to shine in their eyes, seeking constant signs of any approval and affection I could get.

That's where it all started, everything that people who loved me wanted me to do, I did. I got stuck in the people pleasing; I had to do everything to make myself look good in their eyes. If I didn't make things look good in their eyes, I wasn't any good. I ignored everything that I wanted because I had to. I had to make them proud of me because if I didn't, I wasn't worth it. It took me a long time to realize.

My research affirmed my beliefs about my behavior:

"The analysis of my family dynamic—emotional distance, lack of praise, and the pressure to perform—aligns with research on how inconsistent or conditional affection breeds 'people-pleasing' and low self-worth. Without unconditional validation, children internalize the belief that they must earn love by meeting external expectations. This manifests in adulthood as hypervigilance for others' approval, chronic self-sacrifice, and difficulty recognizing or advocating for personal needs, all classic expressions of a wounded inner child and entrenched neural self-criticism."

When I was thirteen, I suffered my first big loss in life when my father passed away. He had heart disease for about a year, and never told my Mom how serious his condition was. We never realized until he passed away from a massive heart attack. In those days, they didn't have a bypass procedure. The only thing he could do was take nitroglycerin pills and hope for the best. He went for a blood-thinning procedure in the hospital two weeks before he passed away. But obviously, that had no real effect. He was only 53 when he passed.

At the time, my oldest brother was in the naval reserve, so he wouldn't get drafted to Vietnam, and my other brother was still in college. Within two years after my father's passing, both my brothers got married, so my mom and I were the only ones left living in the family home.

At first, we clung to each other in grief. She took a break from working for a while, which was not necessarily a good move. She began drinking heavily as I was starting to date and have outside interests, and she became desperately lonely. At the same time, she was having some relationship problems with her side of our family, which was making her even more depressed. My mom never socialized, had very few friends, none of whom were particularly close, and the isolation made her emotionally dependent on me.

The research about this part of my life produced the following:

The premature loss of my father and the dissolution of my immediate family represent profound attachment ruptures. Grief and subsequent parental withdrawal can place adolescents in a "parentified" role, leading to hyper-responsibility and emotional enmeshment. Often, this stunts intuitive self-trust as the child learns to prioritize another's emotional needs over their somatic signals—a phenomenon linked to dissociation and impaired interoceptive awareness in traumatized populations.

Chapter Two

How Your Inner Child Shows Up in Adult Life (Getting Stuck)

One of the most damaging things that can happen to a child is having their basic beliefs about the world shattered. Children naturally create ideas about how life should work based on what they see and experience. They might believe that if they're good, good things will happen to them, or that the adults will always keep their promises. When these beliefs get crushed repeatedly—through broken promises, disappointments, or harsh realities—it creates a deep wound in the child's sense of safety and trust.

This kind of disappointment becomes especially intense during the teenage years. Adolescents start having more sophisticated hopes and dreams about their future, their relationships, and how the world should treat them. When reality doesn't match these expectations, through heartbreak, failures, or simply discovering that life isn't fair, it can fundamentally change how they approach life going forward.

Many people respond to these crushing disappointments by building walls around themselves. They stop dreaming big, stop taking emotional risks, and become much more cautious about opening their hearts. While this protects them from further disappointment, it also cuts them off from the joy and possibility that made childhood so vibrant. They begin to lose their inner child.

One of the most significant changes that happens after childhood disillusionment is that people stop playing and start protecting themselves. Think about how freely children play—they're creative, spontaneous, and willing to try new things without worrying about looking foolish or failing. But when children experience too much disappointment or pain, they often abandon this playful approach to life.

Neurologically, this period involves continued myelination of neural pathways, which speeds transmission but makes established patterns harder to change, like deep ruts in a country road that become increasingly difficult to escape. Our brain's default mode network (DMN) becomes more entrenched, potentially locking in habitual thought patterns that suppress childlike qualities.

Instead of letting their natural curiosity guide them, they start making decisions based on past hurts and fears. They stop asking "What would be fun?" and start asking "What's safe?" This isn't just a behavior change—it's a change in how their brain works. The brain starts prioritizing survival and protection over exploration and growth.

This shift has huge implications for adult life. When your brain is constantly focused on avoiding danger and protecting itself from potential harm, it becomes much harder to adapt to new situations, form close relationships, or pursue personal growth. You end up living a smaller, more cautious life, even when that caution is no longer necessary.

The behaviors and responses we learned as children become deeply embedded in our brain's wiring. These patterns were often the best strategies we could come up with as kids to handle difficult situations, but they frequently don't work well in adult life. The problem is that these neural pathways become so established during childhood that they continue operating automatically, even when we consciously know they're not helpful anymore.

For example, many adults struggle with things like:

- Fear of being abandoned or rejected.
- Difficulty committing to relationships or goals.
- Trouble setting healthy boundaries with others.
- Difficulty asking for what they need or want.

These aren't character flaws—they're protective strategies that made sense when we were children but now get in the way of healthy adult relationships and personal fulfillment. Because these patterns operate below our conscious awareness, we often find ourselves reacting in ways that surprise or frustrate us.

Many adults find themselves stuck in cycles that seem to repeat the same problems. Someone who learned to avoid conflict as a child might find themselves unable to speak up for themselves as an adult, even when it would benefit them. Someone who was criticized heavily might become a perfectionist who's never satisfied with their efforts.

These repetitive patterns happen because the neural pathways established in childhood become like superhighways in our brain—information travels along them quickly and automatically. Even when we intellectually understand that we're repeating unhelpful patterns, our brain defaults to these familiar routes because they feel safe and predictable.

Breaking these patterns requires more than just willpower or positive thinking. It requires creating new neural pathways while also addressing the original wounds that keep pulling us back to the old patterns. This is why inner child work can be so powerful—it helps us understand where these patterns came from and gives us tools to create healthier responses.

One of the clearest signs that someone has a wounded inner child is the presence of a harsh inner critic—that voice in your head that constantly judges, criticizes, and finds fault with everything you do. This critical voice often sounds like the harsh adults from our childhood, and it can become so automatic that we don't even notice it's there.

This inner critic isn't just annoying self-talk—it represents changes in the brain's wiring that happened in response to childhood experiences. When children are frequently criticized, blamed, or made to feel inadequate, their brains adapt by developing this internal monitoring system that tries to catch and prevent mistakes before they happen.

The problem is that this inner critic often becomes more harmful than helpful. Instead of protecting us from real dangers, it undermines our confidence, creativity, and willingness to take healthy risks. It can make us second-guess ourselves constantly and prevent us from pursuing opportunities or relationships that could bring genuine happiness.

Research shows that our inner child, shaped by early experiences, continues to influence how we handle stress, form relationships, and navigate life challenges throughout our entire lives. When the inner child has been wounded by toxic environments, difficult relationships, or repeated disappointments, these wounds create lasting patterns in both our brain structure and our behavior.

The good news is that understanding these patterns is the first step toward healing them. When we recognize that our adult struggles often stem from childhood adaptations, we can approach ourselves with more compassion and begin the work of creating healthier patterns. Our brains remain capable of change throughout our lives, which means it's never too late to heal old wounds and develop new ways of responding to life's challenges.

The inner child isn't just a psychological concept—it's a real part of how our brains work, carrying forward both the wounds and the wisdom from our earliest experiences. By understanding and healing these patterns, we can reclaim the joy, creativity, and openness that are our birthright while also maintaining the wisdom and capabilities we've developed as adults.

Case Studies

Lisa's Story

Unlike many peers, Lisa didn't have clear career aspirations growing up. Her main goal was to "get away from my parents and experience the world unencumbered." She briefly considered occupational therapy after volunteering with Special Olympics, recognizing her natural gift for helping others, but fear of her own powerful emotions led her to suppress this calling.

Before college, Lisa had a recurring vision of herself walking up airplane steps, smartly dressed, waving goodbye, and flying to speak to large crowds. She intuitively knew she was meant for public speaking, though she didn't understand what form it would take.

Choosing between occupational therapy and fashion merchandising, Lisa selected the Fashion Institute of Technology. After graduation, she worked in the garment district, progressing from purchasing to sales, eventually becoming a national sales manager for the children's clothing company Ozona, traveling internationally.

At 27, Lisa married her first husband, a television producer 20 years her senior, whom she met through family connections (he was her great-grandmother's best friend's grandson). They lived in a SoHo loft, and while he was somewhat controlling, he supported her career transition by refusing to simply give her a job in television production.

He insisted Lisa research and apply for a production assistant position herself, saying, "You want to work in television production? Go do the research... You go do it." This approach proved beneficial, as Lisa excelled in production work, eventually earning associate producer credit and discovering she was "capable of just about anything if I put my mind to it."

While working a temporary assignment, Lisa met another Lisa at Time Warner who worked for the vice president of a prominent record label. This connection led to a meeting with a songwriter who needed someone to manage her recording studio. Despite knowing nothing about studio management, Lisa boldly said, "Yes, me. I'd love to work with you."

This transition into the music industry work represents Lisa reconnecting with her authentic self—the confident, capable person who could see the whole picture and rise to any occasion. She reflects that "it's that same girl that needs to get out there in my business now... Reclaim that person that I was."

Although she sometimes got carried away with the excitement of New York's fast-paced environment, she was also growing tired of New York's "underbelly," expensive alternate-side parking, and the challenges of city life with a dog.

Lisa decided to make a change. Her lifelong friends, who had been her classmates from first grade through 11th grade, had moved to Virginia after graduating high school early. They would visit during President's Day weekends, and Lisa would take the train down to see them.

When one of them offered to rent her townhouse to Lisa, she initially hesitated and "chickened out." A year later, when the other tenant moved out, Lisa committed to the move. However, family obligations delayed her departure by two weeks, creating financial stress since she was living paycheck to paycheck.

On July 3, 1999, Lisa drove a truck with all her belongings to Virginia, with her boyfriend following in her car with her dog. She vowed never to move herself again, declaring she would hire professionals next time.

Lisa quickly found recruiting work in Virginia's telecom corridor in Northern Virginia. She loved having her townhouse and living near her lifelong friends, plus making new friends, who all remain close to this day.

Her recruiting career spanned from New York to Virginia, nearly 25 years total. She became a subject matter expert in IT recruiting, supporting government contracts for federal agencies and even some intelligence community projects. During this period, she also worked for global corporations, describing this as her "growing up" phase—though she notes she was simultaneously on a spiritual journey, having considered coaching for 20 years before actually pursuing it.

Lisa met Brad through workplace social events organized by colleagues. Brad was a coworker of someone she was dating, and they met at group outings—Indian food dinners, Arabic cuisine, camping trips, and cycling events. Initially drawn to cycling to lose the 25 pounds she'd gained after moving from New York's walking culture to Virginia's car-dependent lifestyle, Lisa found herself increasingly drawn to Brad.

He was intelligent, knowledgeable about many subjects, and had coached the women's cycling team at a university, where he worked as a systems administrator. Through cycling training and conversations, Lisa discovered her feelings for Brad were stronger than she could have ever imagined. "One day, it kind of hit me over the head like a hammer. Like, oh my God, I think I love this guy," she recalls.

After about three years of getting to know each other, they got married, and Lisa bought her first townhouse in her name, wanting to prove to herself that she could be a homeowner and "grownup."

Brad was diabetic and didn't manage his condition well despite Lisa's efforts to encourage healthy eating and lifestyle changes. She recognized she couldn't control his choices, stating, "I wasn't his mother, and I didn't tell him what to do that much."

Their final year together was complicated by Lisa's mother moving in temporarily while transitioning to Florida, and Brad's declining health. He began having dangerous blood sugar highs and lows, and Lisa believes he knew he was dying when he started writing prose during a New Year's visit to family in Roanoke.

In early 2013, Brad developed an infection that progressed to gangrene and sepsis. The week of Lisa's 50th birthday, she realized he was seriously ill and was hospitalized at the VA medical center in Washington, D.C.—an experience Lisa found traumatic due to the facility's condition and her fears about the quality of care.

Brad came home with a port for IV medication and required wound care, which Lisa administered. Despite the amputation, his condition worsened. One Monday morning, one month after Lisa's 50th birthday, Brad collapsed while trying to get to the bathroom. Lisa called 911, knowing he was gone, but the hospital kept him on life support for 72 hours.

The trauma of Brad's death, combined with managing her mother's needs and the stress of maintaining her recruiting job, eventually overwhelmed Lisa. She went on disability a year and a half later, unable to think clearly or perform her job duties.

Brad's death marked the beginning of Lisa's transformational journey—her "do-over at 50." She describes seeing "the light go out of him" and recognizes this as a pivotal moment that changed everything about her life's direction.

This story captures Lisa's journey from early trauma and suppressed intuition to gradual reclamation of her authentic self, setting the stage for her eventual transformation into the empowered coach and speaker she envisioned in her childhood.

* * *

Jane's Story

"Due to strong aptitude test results, I initially pursued engineering because it seemed 'safe'—a blue-collar mentality from my hometown, even though my father was an accountant. The program nearly killed me mentally and almost caused me to fail out of university. I desperately wanted to pursue sports management, but lacked the confidence to advocate for myself, though I believe my family would have supported me if I had.

After six months, I switched to geography with a concentration in international trade, which gave me a perspective on different cultures and viewpoints. I researched industrial location, interviewing companies in the local area and across the border in Canada. This degree was created in partnership with the business community, which provided practical experience.

I fell into insurance through a part-time job my sister helped me get. I stayed in the industry not out of passion, but because I didn't think I could do anything else. Even when moving countries with my ex-husband (partly as escapism from where I was in life), I returned to insurance because it felt safe during a recession.

Throughout my insurance career, I experienced repeated patterns of being overlooked and undermined. While on maternity leave, they hired a new office manager who told me upon my return that I was "lucky to be back" and that upper management wasn't happy with me. This occurred during what I now recognize was likely postpartum depression, and I didn't question her authority for six to eight months until she was eventually let go. It wasn't until much later, when having an unrelated conversation with someone at the Director level, that the former office manager's feedback was untrue.

Eventually, I was loaned to a head office position in the high-net-worth market, where I stayed because I lacked the confidence to venture out on my own.

The pattern repeated itself three times—getting burnt out, facing ethical conflicts, having opportunities taken away, and being let go during company restructuring. I couldn't show up as my full self because my sense of humor and personality were often met with disdain. It felt safer to keep parts of myself hidden.

After the third time being let go, I realized I was the common denominator. This wasn't about blame—it was about recognizing that I needed something different. The universe had to close doors for me because I wasn't getting the message on my own.

Reluctantly, I called my ex-husband for advice. Despite not wanting to involve him, we shared a daughter with university expenses ahead. He listened quietly and said he would get back to me. He connected me with someone who does what I do now and even provided a microloan for the training. I had to undergo the same process as my clients do now.

Through this process, I began to understand the stories I had told myself since childhood that created these patterns. I learned to identify what I was holding onto and how to create a new reality for myself.

The transformation included recognizing how fear-based my decisions had been. As my mother later observed, I 'never had confidence' and 'always seemed scared.' I had been running my adult life based on decisions I made when I was four or five years old."

Jane's hesitation to follow her interests and her eventual choice of "safe" career paths show how early expectations and emotional environments develop core limiting beliefs about competence, safety, and self-advocacy. These beliefs—often based on childhood role interpretations (like "don't be a bother," "keep the peace")—influence later decisions, risk-taking, and the ability to assert needs both professionally and personally. Her mother's later remark that Jane "never had confidence" highlights how such stories are reinforced over time.

Jane's experience of chronic undervaluation, workplace undermining, and burnout illustrates the repetition compulsion described in psychodynamic theory: people unconsciously recreate familiar emotional patterns from childhood in their adult lives, seeking mastery or resolution. When Jane repeatedly feels overlooked or disrespected, it mirrors internalized childhood scripts of invisibility and inadequacy—a pattern well-documented to stem from early emotional neglect or over-adaptation.

"In relationships, I couldn't advocate for myself and would always submit. I'd hide parts of my personality, then years later get rejected for putting myself on the back burner. I only realized in the past ten years that I had trouble making eye contact and couldn't remember people's faces because I kept my eyes averted.

I spent years making myself smaller, taking on other people's emotions to avoid upsetting anyone, and remaining in a reactive state. I wanted to do everything myself but refused help, then felt resentful when no one assisted me—a cycle I couldn't break because I didn't know how to ask for what I needed."

Jane's inability to advocate for herself in relationships, her tendency to hide parts of her personality, avert her eyes, and avoid asking for help are classic signs of insecure or anxious attachment styles. Such adults may remain conflict-avoidant, hypervigilant to others' needs, and reluctant to reveal anything that could disrupt group harmony; this aligns with the literature on survivors of "developmental" or "complex" trauma, whose boundaries and sense of self-agency are often chronically compromised.

* * *

My Story

Because of the climate at home, I was not excited about going to college. I was apathetic about my course of study. My mom forbade me from going away to college, and I was beginning to become depressed myself. I didn't know it at the time. All I knew was I wanted to get out of the house.

When I graduated from high school, I decided to take a year off and work for a year. I graduated from high school after only three years through an accelerated program. During my last year, I was in school for 12 months, and I wanted a break. I went to work on Wall Street in Manhattan at an international bank. This was a great new experience, and I enjoyed new friendships, earning money, and feeling independent.

In the meantime, I applied to attend Rutgers University the following Fall. I started learning all about psychology because my brother's a psychologist. He's a clinical psychologist. Well, he was, he's retired now.

I loved listening to him talk about it. At the time, he was attending Rutgers for a Ph.D. I started studying it. There were a lot of hippies on campus; they wore jeans and beards, and they would stand up and mouth off to the professor. After working in the straight-laced corporate world for a year, I was like, whoa, this is not right. I've got to get out of here. This is so funny because if it were today, I'd be perfectly happy.

I left after three months. I left and I went back to work, and I did all my schooling at night. I studied business, earned a BBA at Pace University, and later an MBA from Pace.

In the meantime, while I was working and earning my BBA, I got married at 23. When I graduated with my BBA, I went to work for a technology company as a computer systems designer. In those days, companies paid for their employees' graduate education, so I started earning my MBA almost immediately. After earning my MBA in marketing, by this time I had switched from computers to marketing, and as a strategic market planner, I expected a promotion.

This was when I first experienced gender discrimination in the workplace. At the same time, my husband and I bought a small meat and grocery store, which my husband managed. My boss, at the time, made the biggest mistake he could ever have made by saying to my office mate in a private conversation, "Why should I promote her? She is only going to get pregnant and leave anyway. She and her husband just bought a store, and she's not going to have to work. I'm giving the promotion to so and so because he just had a kid, and he needs it."

I resigned from the company. My husband and I separated that summer and eventually divorced.

After leaving the tech company after seven years of working there, I began working for a technology consulting company in Manhattan as a research manager.

About a year later, the company was acquired by a major publishing firm.

My immediate boss, the director of the research practice I managed, resigned, and I was promoted to director.

Shortly after, cost cuts were putting people's heads on the chopping block.

Instead of acting ethically, they started making up false accusations and misconstruing events. One person, a good friend of mine, was targeted and terminated. She sued the company for wrongful dismissal and unpaid commissions. She won.

I was their next target. They began to exercise abusive tactics to get me to resign. I went home sick one day and never returned. My doctor signed an affidavit that I could not return because the workplace was a toxic environment.

They gave me a compensation package. While working at this company, I remarried and moved to another state, which made the commute to Manhattan unbearable anyway. So, I guess the universe did me a favor in the long run.

My research produced the following about this part of my life:

My later experiences in the workplace—gender discrimination, toxic environments, and the persistent drive to please and perform—demonstrate the endurance of childhood neural and psychological patterns into adult life. Workplace adversity triggered formal depression and ultimately a reckoning with authentic needs versus conditioned behaviors. This aligns with research showing that childhood adversity sets up neurobiological patterns where adults may unconsciously recreate familiar toxic dynamics in new settings until the underlying wounds are addressed.

Chapter Three

The Journey of the Inner Child: From Loss to Rediscovery (Getting Unstuck)

Around midlife, many of us experience a renewed interest in finding our lost inner child. This often coincides with what Jung called "individuation" - the process of integrating different aspects of ourselves into something more whole and authentic.

Several factors might trigger this rediscovery:

1. Achievement of external goals creates space for looking inward. Once we've climbed the mountain, we have time to notice the flowers along the path.
2. Recognition of our mortality prompts reflection on what truly brings joy. The ticking clock makes us question whether spreadsheets are more important than finger painting after all.
3. Exposure to younger generations reawakens our playful instincts. Nothing brings back your inner child like building a sandcastle with a four-year-old.
4. Life transitions create opportunities for reevaluation. Sometimes we need to get knocked sideways to see what's been beside us all along.

Neurologically, our aging brain shows interesting changes that might help us reconnect with our inner child. While overall neural plasticity decreases, our brain demonstrates "dedifferentiation" - a breaking down of specialized boundaries that allows for more integrated processing. This might enable a better balance between logical left-brain and creative right-brain functions.

Research suggests older adults often show reduced self-consciousness and better emotional regulation, allowing greater freedom to express childlike qualities without fear of judgment. There's also a shift in perspective that prioritizes emotional meaning over achievement - what psychologist Laura Carstensen calls "socioemotional selectivity." We stop worrying so much about appearances and start caring more about authenticity.

Modern psychology offers various paths back to our inner child:

1. Inner child therapy techniques involve dialoging with our younger self through visualization or journaling - essentially calling out to the lost spirit within us.
2. Play therapy principles have been adapted for adults to facilitate emotional expression and spontaneity, permitting ourselves to play again.
3. Mindfulness practices help us observe thoughts without judgment, creating space for authentic expression.
4. Creative arts therapies provide channels for expression that bypass logical defenses, allowing our inner child to dance across the road rather than freezing in the headlights like a deer.

These approaches create new neural pathways, essentially "rewiring" our brain to integrate childlike qualities with adult wisdom. Neuroplasticity makes this integration possible even later in life, though it requires consistent practice and intention.

The journey of our inner child - from natural expression in childhood, through suppression in adulthood, to rediscovery later in life - represents a path to wholeness. By reclaiming the spontaneity and emotional authenticity of our inner child while maintaining the wisdom of maturity, we achieve a more integrated sense of self.

The neurological underpinnings show the remarkable adaptability of our brain across the lifespan. While certain developmental windows close, our brain maintains capacity for change throughout life, allowing us to rediscover our inner child as part of our continuing journey. Like a deer crossing the dark country road, our inner child may get momentarily stunned by life's challenges, but with patience and care, it can rejoin the family waiting on the other side.

Case Studies

Lisa's Story

Six months after Brad's death, following advice from Brad's best friend to "get out of your house and go do something like a hobby," Lisa remembered her love of music and decided to attend a local open mic night. Inspired by an invitation from a former coworker and friend who performed there and was a talented musician.

Now, seeing Mike perform, Lisa was amazed by his musical talent and the quality of the open mic community, which became Lisa's lifeline, pulling her out of her "grieving funk" and isolation. She had been struggling with fundamental questions: "Why am I still here? What am I supposed to be doing? What is my life going to look like now?"

Despite Mike's obvious growing interest, Lisa resisted a romantic relationship, telling him, "you don't want this" and "you don't know what you think you want." She wasn't ready to relinquish her connection to Brad, still feeling married in her heart and mind.

After six months of attending the open mic and gradually building their connection, Lisa realized this was "something important that I need to pay attention to." She recognized that the universe had brought them back together for a reason.

Even though there was no shared history to justify it, Lisa and Mike had "auto-trust built in"—a deep confidence in each other that came from being "older and wiser and experienced in life." This foundation allowed them to build a relationship that would be "completely different" from anything either had experienced before.

Lisa's life in Virginia was marked by multiple significant losses:

- Her grandmother, followed by her beloved golden retriever, died a week later.
- Her stepfather's passing.
- One of her aunts' deaths, shortly after Brad passed.
- Her brother-in-law's death the following year.
- Being scammed out of money during this vulnerable period.

Mike also experienced profound loss during the first year of their marriage when his son died of pancreatic cancer, adding another layer of shared grief to their bond.

Lisa had considered coaching throughout her recruiting career for at least 20 years before finally attending the Health Coach Institute.

This story captures Lisa's journey from career success through devastating loss to spiritual awakening and new love.

* * *

Jane's Story

"Now I have greater self-awareness and understand how others communicate, allowing me to adapt my communication style accordingly. I recognize that it's my responsibility to make myself understood, not others' responsibility to understand me.

While I still occasionally fall into old patterns, I now have tools to recognize them earlier and get myself out of these cycles more quickly. The growth process took time—I needed to go through it when I was ready to hear it."

Jane's turning point—realizing she is the "common denominator" and exploring the root stories from childhood—corresponds with what academic sources call **narrative integration** and "inner child work." Identifying and challenging longstanding patterns, acquiring new skills (communication, boundary-setting), and developing self-compassion are recognized in trauma research as the chief agents of transformation and adult growth. The fact that Jane is now able to recognize old triggers and intervene sooner aligns closely with post-traumatic growth frameworks: change is possible when there is insight, readiness, and supportive interpersonal environments.

***

My Story

When I left the technology company, I began to awaken to the possibility that my authentic self was wrongly served by working in my occupation and in these environments. After this experience at the technology consulting company, I intuitively knew that I needed a change, but I still chose to ignore the signals. I continued to tell myself that I just needed a new job, but I needed a complete change.

Another fact that made it difficult for me to make a change was that, from an ego standpoint, I had a fantastic salary, top health, vacation, and investment benefits. Why would I want anything else? This was the internal battle going on for years.

It was clearly evident to me that this battle started because my intuition and my inner child were coming alive again.

When I left the technology consulting company, I did a couple of short gigs at local consulting companies, which were great, but I knew at the get-go that they were going to be temporary contracts, and I was happy with that.

My research produced the following about this part of my life:

My later experiences in the workplace—gender discrimination, toxic environments, and the persistent drive to please and perform—demonstrate the endurance of childhood neural and psychological patterns into adult life.

Workplace adversity triggered formal depression and ultimately a reckoning with authentic needs versus conditioned behaviors. This aligns with research showing that childhood adversity sets up neurobiological patterns where adults may unconsciously recreate familiar toxic dynamics in new settings until the underlying wounds are addressed.

Last, but not least, I spent the last two years of my corporate career at another technology consulting company as a research director. I remember when I accepted the position, I said to myself, "What are you doing?" But the universe put me there, and I'm so glad it did.

In this last position of my corporate career, I was walking down the hallway one day, and my boss's boss was walking from the other direction with his executive coach.

He introduced me to her, and we began to chat. We stood there and talked for about 10 minutes. She and I talked, and he walked away because we were busy talking, but the light bulbs just totally went off in my head.

It was like, whoa, this is what I want to do. That's when it all started. That's when my whole life started to change.

At the time, my husband and I were trying to get pregnant. I was going through all sorts of fertility treatments, and I was in my early forties. It all eventually worked out. After having my girls, I went to the Institute for Professional Excellence in Coaching (iPEC) when they were seven. When I graduated a year later from coaching school, I tried to practice for about a year, but I couldn't because it was just too overwhelming with my eight-year-old twin daughters. In 2021, when they were in college, I started my practice again.

Chapter Four

The Relationship of Your Inner Child To Your Intuition

Have you ever had a strong "gut feeling" about something—maybe sensing that someone wasn't trustworthy or knowing the right answer without being able to explain why? This ability, called intuition, is deeply connected to your childhood experiences and what psychologists call your "inner child."

Intuition is your brain's ability to understand or know something without having to think it through logically. It turns out that this skill develops from the same brain systems that handle childhood learning and emotions. Your inner child, which holds all your childhood emotional experiences and patterns, either helps or hurts your ability to use intuition, depending on what kind of childhood you had.

This connection works through three main ways: your brain keeps using the thinking patterns you developed as a young child, your early relationships get "wired" into your brain, and your intuitive abilities remain flexible throughout your life based on those childhood experiences.

When you were a young child (roughly ages 4-7), your brain worked very differently than it does now. During this stage, described by psychologist Jean Piaget, children rely on what he called "intuitive thought"—they understand things through overall impressions and feelings rather than step-by-step logical thinking.

During these early years, the right side of your brain dominates, which specializes in recognizing patterns, processing emotions, and imaginative play. These are all key parts of how intuition works. The neural pathways formed during this time become the foundation for your adult intuitive abilities, with your inner child acting as a bridge back to this natural way of knowing.

If you had caregivers who were responsive and supportive, this strengthened your connection to intuition. When you had gut feelings as a child, and adults validated those feelings, your brain learned to trust these internal signals. For example, if you instinctively avoided a mean kid at school and your parents supported your choice, your brain reinforced that your gut feelings were valuable and accurate.

This validation creates strong neural pathways connecting your emotional processing center (the amygdala) to the part of your brain that notices what's happening in your body (the insula). These connections allow for faster and more accurate intuitive judgments in adulthood.

If your caregivers regularly dismissed your fears, concerns, or gut feelings, you learned to distrust your internal signals. This causes the related neural networks to weaken over time. As an adult, this might show up as overthinking simple decisions or ignoring physical sensations that warn you of danger—something commonly seen in trauma survivors who report "not being able to trust their gut."

Your ability to use intuition depends heavily on the opportunities you had as a child for unstructured play and emotional connection with caregivers. When children engage in imaginative play, it activates a brain network called the default mode network, which helps create the spontaneous connections that lead to intuitive insights.

Children who are encouraged in imaginative play develop stronger connections between the memory center (hippocampus) and the part of the brain that detects errors and patterns (anterior cingulate cortex). This creates sophisticated pattern recognition abilities—a key feature of expert intuition.

Three Key Factors That Shape Intuitive Development:

1. Validation of Emotional Experiences: When caregivers mirror a child's emotions (saying things like "I see you're scared—that dog does look big!"), they help the child learn to interpret body signals (like increased heart rate) as meaningful, intuitive information.
2. Tolerance for Uncertainty: Children who are allowed to work through minor conflicts on their own develop thicker brain tissue in the area that handles uncertain situations (orbitofrontal cortex), making them more comfortable in ambiguous situations where intuition is most useful.
3. Creative Freedom: Unstructured activities like art or storytelling increase the integrity of the connections between the logical and intuitive parts of the brain, helping them work together better.

Toxic environments create the opposite effects. Chronic stress during childhood elevates stress hormones (cortisol), which prune away neural connections in the memory center and prefrontal cortex—areas essential for making sense of intuitive impulses.

This brain damage shows up in adulthood as "intuitive override," where people dismiss accurate gut feelings because their threat-detection system is distorted. Research found that 73% of adults with childhood trauma had impaired ability to sense what was happening in their bodies compared to people without trauma, and brain scans showed reduced activity in the intuitive processing areas during intuitive tasks.

When a child experiences ongoing trauma, the brain uses a protective strategy called dissociation that cuts off conscious access to intuitive wisdom. The brain essentially creates a "split" between explicit memory (what you consciously remember) and implicit emotional knowledge (what your body knows), protecting the child from overwhelming pain but breaking apart intuitive processing.

This shows up in adults as:

- Body Disconnection: Inability to interpret bodily signals (like not recognizing hunger until feeling faint).
- Emotional Numbness: Having a flat emotional response despite subconsciously detecting threats accurately (like "knowing" a partner is being unfaithful but feeling nothing about it).
- Creativity Loss: Losing spontaneous creativity and flexible problem-solving abilities.

These protective adaptations create "intuitive blind spots" where people repeatedly enter harmful situations despite subconsciously being aware of the danger. Brain scans show these patterns correlate with overactivity in the rumination network and weakened connections to the threat-detection network.

The good news is that therapeutic work focused on healing the inner child can restore intuitive abilities by rebuilding the severed neural connections.

Several effective approaches include:

1. Reparenting Visualizations: Guided imagery exercises where adults mentally comfort their childhood selves activate the brain region associated with perspective-taking (temporoparietal junction). Brain imaging studies show these practices increase connections between the emotional center (amygdala) and the emotional regulation area (medial prefrontal cortex), improving emotional balance during intuitive decision-making.
2. Embodied Play Therapy: When adults engage in childlike play (like sandbox work or improvisational theater), it stimulates the brain's creative centers while quieting the critical judgment areas. This creates a brain state similar to the theta brainwaves seen in children during intuitive learning, making it easier to generate insights.
3. Body Awareness Practice: Mindfulness practices that focus on bodily sensations rebuild connections in the insula (the body-awareness center). A 12-week program of daily body scan meditation increased intuitive accuracy by 41% in adults with childhood trauma, and brain scans showed increased gray matter density in the anterior insula.
4. Creative Journaling: Writing with your non-dominant hand activates the right hemisphere's intuitive networks while bypassing the left hemisphere's analytical censorship. Clients who journaled about traumatic memories with their non-dominant hand demonstrated 30% greater access to subconscious intuitive solutions compared to traditional talk therapy alone.

Long-term studies confirm that intuition can be rebuilt well into adulthood. People in inner child therapy programs showed 14% improvement in intuition (measured by decision-making tasks) after 6 months, with the improvements lasting at least 18 months later. Brain imaging revealed these improvements matched with restored connections in the neural pathway (uncinate fasciculus) that connects emotional memory centers to the prefrontal areas that regulate emotions.

This brain flexibility shows that the inner child continues to serve as an intuitive reservoir throughout life. Even people who experienced severe trauma can reclaim their intuitive wisdom by reprocessing childhood experiences through modern therapeutic techniques. As the inner child heals, the brain's natural ability to turn subconscious knowledge into conscious insight is restored—a process clients often describe as "learning to hear my soul's whisper again."

Your inner child isn't just a psychological concept from the past—it's an active part of your current neurological system that preserves the intuitive abilities you developed during critical childhood years. Its "whispers" come through your gut's nervous system, your heart's nervous system, and your brain's default network, providing continuous guidance that adults often override through unhelpful coping strategies.

Modern neuroscience now confirms what depth psychologists have long believed: healing the inner child through repairing attachment wounds, engaging in creative expression, and developing body awareness unlocks intuitive abilities that go beyond logical thinking. For those willing to revisit and heal their childhood emotional experiences, the reward is nothing less than reconnecting with their innate wisdom—a wisdom that knows before it thinks, guided by the unbroken child within.

The relationship between your inner child and your intuition is one of the most profound connections in human psychology. By understanding and healing this relationship, you can reclaim access to a powerful source of guidance that has been with you since birth, waiting patiently for you to remember how to listen.

Case Studies

Lisa's Story

Before the abuse occurred, between the ages of 10-13, Lisa had a profound spiritual experience while sitting on a rock at the beach, feeling "connected to everything." This early awakening to her intuitive abilities was later suppressed by trauma.

The sexual abuse by her stepfather and her mother's inability to protect her reinforce deep patterns of betrayal trauma, helplessness, and silencing of the inner child.

* * *

Jane's Story

"This journey has enabled me to help other women fully show up as themselves, something I wasn't able to do for most of my life. While I wish I had gone through this transformation decades earlier, I had to experience it when I was ready to receive and incorporate the lessons."

Finally, Jane's desire to help other women step into their authentic selves exemplifies the movement from "surviving" to "thriving," a trajectory well-documented in trauma and resilience literature. This process is seen as both a healing mechanism ("what I couldn't do for myself, I can help others do") and evidence of reclaiming the "exiled" or wounded parts of the self—the heart of inner child healing.

* * *

My Story

The Akashic records show that I lived a few lives before this one, and both my warrior archetype and my empathy, which drives me to seek justice, were present then as well as today. From the day I was born into this life, these traits were strongly present. The way I came into this world proved I was ready to battle for my life!

As the story was told to me, when I arrived home from the hospital, my brothers, ages six and eight, were full of wide-eyed wonder at this little creature, only five pounds, like a bag of flour. Yet I had tiny hands and little feet that moved, and I made tiny noises like cooing and even made big noises when I cried. Although I was not mentally cognizant of the world around me, I'm sure my intuitive spirit shone through my tiny, bright eyes. I was here to learn something, and like a little sponge, I began to absorb every sense, every detail of this new world.

On the first day of kindergarten, I couldn't understand why so many of the children were crying when their mothers left them for the day. I remember being perfectly calm and couldn't wait to explore the classroom. I've been a lifelong learner from that first day, and as I write this, I realize my sense of independence grew from there. My love of learning flowed continually throughout my life. My inner child was a curious explorer filled with wonder from the start.

My research indicates that these early years established my core of healthy inner child experiences. This healthy foundation strengthened my ability to rely on my intuition and maintain a strong sense of self during periods of adversity later in life.

Unbeknownst to anybody, a year after my first husband and I bought the meat and grocery store, we started having marital problems. The pressure between work and home threw me into depression.

Being formally diagnosed with depression, I went out on disability leave for about six weeks. Upon returning to work, I resigned.

Therapy sessions during this time made me realize that I had lost my inner child through these challenging experiences. In fact, I remember my therapist saying to me, "You've lost all your spirit."

For a few years, I felt apathetic about everything. My sense of self-trust eroded, my confidence deflated, and I felt like a lost soul.

When I left the technology company, I began to awaken to the possibility that my authentic self was wrongly served by being in my occupation and working in these types of environments. After this experience at the technology consulting company, I intuitively knew that I needed a change, but I still chose to ignore the signals. I continued to tell myself that I just needed a new job, but I needed a complete change.

Another fact that made it difficult for me to make a change was that, from an ego standpoint, I had a fantastic salary, top health, vacation, and investment benefits. Why would I want anything else? This was the internal battle going on for years.

It wasn't until I left corporate life for good that I chose to let my intuition take the reins once again and lead me to a better way of life.

In 2007, I began my education in life coaching. My professional coach certification completely changed my outlook on life as I rediscovered my inner child.

Chapter Five

The Unconscious Mind – Your Hidden Brilliance

A Conversation with Master Coach Jill Tomczak-Redman

One of the most powerful insights about neuroplasticity and intuition comes from understanding how our unconscious mind actually works. To explore this deeper, I want to share the wisdom of Jill Tomczak-Redman, a Master Results Coach, Board Certified Trainer of Hypnosis and Neuro-Linguistic Programming (NLP), and Head of two institutes specializing in the conscious mind, unconscious mind, and higher self.

Jill's work illuminates something crucial: the neural pathways we've been discussing don't just affect how we think; they affect our access to our own intuitive brilliance. Here's what she wants you to understand.

* * *

Here's something most people don't realize: the solution to whatever is stopping you already exists. Right now. Inside you.

It's sitting there in your unconscious mind, waiting to be accessed. The problem isn't that you don't have the answer; it's that somewhere along the way, you built a wall between yourself and your own brilliance.

Let me explain.

When you were young, somewhere between birth and about seven years old, you lived in your unconscious mind 24/7. You had your imagination running wild. You had imaginary friends. You became imaginary characters. You saw things others couldn't see. Many of us saw auras. We talked to people who weren't there. We just knew things without knowing how we knew them.

This wasn't make-believe. This was you living fully connected to your intuition, your knowing, your higher self.

Then something happened.

You got older. You started creating a barrier between your conscious mind and your unconscious mind. Think of it like an iceberg, your conscious mind is just the tip above the water, while your unconscious mind is the massive part underneath. And separating the two is something called the critical faculty.

When you're young, that critical faculty is porous. It allows you to travel back and forth easily between your conscious and unconscious mind. You can access that intuition, that brilliance, that connection to something greater than yourself.

But then people started telling you things.

"That's not normal." "That's not right." "You're making people uncomfortable."

So you started clamping it down. You began to color inside the lines. Trees were no longer pink; now they had to be brown and green. Your imagination got smaller. Your connection got weaker. That critical faculty became less porous, more rigid, more closed.

And bit by bit, you lost access to your own brilliance.

This is neuroplasticity in action, but working against you. Your brain literally rewired itself to shut down your intuitive access in response to external pressure and criticism.

Here's what most people don't understand: your unconscious mind is the part of you that drives you without you having to think about it.

It's the part that gets you up in the middle of the night and guides you exactly where you need to go, even in the dark. It's what gets the coffee brewing in the morning before you're fully awake. It's what drives you home when you arrive and think, "Wait, how did I get here?" that driving trance we all know.

This is brilliance. This is your unconscious mind running the show.

And this is exactly what we want to tap into more often, because here's the thing: you're already in a trance about ninety percent of your day anyway. So why not access the part of you that knows what to do, that says the right words, does the right things in front of the right people, and recognizes opportunities despite yourself?

Your higher self, that perfect blueprint for health, that source of inspiration, that God spark within you, talks to your unconscious mind. And your unconscious mind talks to your conscious mind.

But your thinking mind? Your conscious, rational, analytical mind? It doesn't talk to your higher self. There's no direct connection there.

The unconscious mind is the conduit. It's the bridge. And if we can keep that bridge open and free, we're getting that perfection, that guidance, that divine inspiration flowing through us.

This is what real intuition is. This is what "knowing without knowing" means.

Now, sometimes your unconscious mind creates blocks. And it does this to protect you.

Let's say something happened to you. Maybe you went in front of a room to speak, and you froze. Or you got sick. Something traumatized you about speaking in front of people. Your unconscious mind took note of that pain, that fear, that discomfort.

And it made a decision: "No, you're not going to do that ever again."

That decision is now in your neurology. It's running in the background, protecting you from that perceived danger. Your unconscious mind thinks it's helping you, but in reality, it's blocking you from opportunities, from growth, from the very thing you may need to do to move forward.

This is where neuroplasticity becomes our ally. We need to get that unconscious block out. We need to go way back to where that decision was made and update it. We need to rewire that neural pathway and let your unconscious mind know: "I'm safe now. I can do this now. That old protection isn't needed anymore."

The goal isn't to shut down your conscious mind or live completely in a dream state. The goal is to keep that critical faculty porous, to maintain the connection between your conscious and unconscious mind so you can access your brilliance whenever you need it.

When you do this, you're not overthinking. You're not second-guessing. You're not paralyzed by analysis. You're flowing. You're intuitive. You're tapped into that higher guidance that knows exactly what you need to do and when you need to do it.

This is what it means to get out of your own way. This is what it means to trust yourself. This is what it means to live from that place of inner knowing instead of outer noise.

Your unconscious mind has the solutions. It always has. The question is: are you willing to remove the barriers and let that brilliance come through?

* * *

Bringing It Together

Jill's insights show us something profound: our intuition isn't some mystical ability we either have or don't have. It's a natural capacity we all possessed as children, one that got neurologically suppressed through conditioning and criticism.

The good news? What was wired can be rewired. What was closed can be reopened. This is the beautiful intersection of neuroplasticity and intuition—and it's exactly what the work ahead will help you access.

Reflection

Think about a time when you just knew something without knowing how you knew it. A time when you followed your gut and it led you exactly where you needed to go. That was your unconscious mind speaking.

Now think about an area of your life where you feel blocked, stuck, or unable to move forward. What old decision might your unconscious mind have made to protect you? What would change if you could update that decision now?

The solutions are already inside you. Your job is simply to clear the pathway and let them emerge.

To learn more about Jill-Tomczak-Redman:
https://www.linkedin.com/search/results/all/?keywords=Jill+Tomczak-Redman+Coaching+

Part Two

Positive Intelligence (Mental Fitness)

Chapter Six

INTRODUCTION TO MENTAL FITNESS

Mental fitness is a concept that has transformed the way we approach life's challenges. As a transformational life coach and mental fitness trainer—sometimes referred to as a Positive Intelligence coach—I've witnessed firsthand the profound impact this approach can have on people's lives. In this chapter, I'll introduce you to the fundamental concepts of mental fitness and explain how this science-based approach can help you thrive in challenging times.

At its core, mental fitness is your ability to deal with life's challenges with a positive mindset, rather than getting upset and stressed. While this definition may sound simple, the science behind it is both profound and transformative.

The concept of mental fitness, also known as Positive Intelligence, emerged from four major breakthroughs in neuroscience that have developed over the past several decades. These scientific advances have fundamentally changed our understanding of how the brain works and how we can harness its power to improve our lives.

The Four Scientific Breakthroughs

Neuroplasticity

The first breakthrough is the discovery of neuroplasticity—the brain's remarkable ability to change and adapt throughout our lives.

The neural pathways of the brain, which function like the brain's muscles, are constantly growing and evolving. This means you are continually working the muscles of your brain, whether you're aware of it or not. This discovery revolutionized our understanding of the brain, proving that we're not locked into fixed patterns of thinking and behavior.

Positive Psychology

The second breakthrough is positive psychology, which fundamentally challenged previous scientific beliefs. Before positive psychology emerged, the prevailing wisdom was that you needed to achieve success, make accomplishments, and do whatever was necessary to be successful to achieve happiness in your life.

However, positive psychology revealed the opposite to be true: you have to be happy first before you can achieve peak performance, great achievements, and great success in life. This insight has transformed how we approach personal and professional development.

Cognitive Behavioral Psychology

The third scientific foundation is cognitive behavioral psychology. This field revealed that the brain operates with automatic patterns that enforce limiting beliefs—those beliefs that were instilled in us throughout our lives. We are conditioned to have certain beliefs, and if left unchallenged, we will continue to hold these beliefs indefinitely.

Through positive intelligence, we can change these interpretations and limiting beliefs to create new ones. By doing so, the brain develops different responses and different interpretive patterns, freeing us from outdated conditioning.

Performance Science

The fourth breakthrough is performance science, which was originally developed to measure athletes' performance and achievements. This science provides measurable frameworks for understanding and optimizing human performance across all areas of life.

The Work of Mental Fitness Training

As mental fitness trainers or Positive Intelligence coaches, we frame and reframe our clients' life experiences so that they can grow their core mental muscles and thrive in challenging times. This work centers on developing three key mental muscle groups:

Saboteur Interceptors: The first set of core mental muscles involves learning to recognize and intercept your saboteurs—those internal voices and patterns that undermine your success and well-being.

Sage Powers: The second set of mental muscles we develop are what we call sage powers. These are the positive neural pathways that help you respond to challenges with wisdom, creativity, and calm clarity.

Self-Command: The third muscle is self-command—your ability to direct your mind toward constructive rather than destructive patterns, especially in moments of stress or challenge.

The Impact of Mental Fitness

By consistently working these mental muscles, the impact on your life can be substantial and multifaceted:

> Peak Performance: You'll operate at your highest level of capability.

> Peace of Mind: You'll experience greater calm and emotional balance.

Wellness: Your overall well-being will improve.

Healthy Relationships: You'll develop stronger, more fulfilling connections with others.

In my experience, healthy relationships are the area where mental fitness has the most profound impact. When you learn to manage your own mental patterns and respond to life's challenges with greater wisdom and calm, every relationship in your life benefits.

The concepts I've introduced in this chapter provide a foundation for understanding mental fitness. While these principles may seem simple on the surface, their application can be life-changing. As you continue through this book, we'll explore each of these concepts in greater depth, providing you with practical tools and strategies to develop your own mental fitness.

The journey to mental fitness is not about perfection—it's about progress. It's about recognizing that your brain is constantly changing, and you have the power to direct that change in positive, life-affirming directions. Whether you're facing professional challenges, personal difficulties, or simply seeking to live a more fulfilling life, mental fitness provides a roadmap for thriving rather than merely surviving.

Chapter Seven

SABOTAGING BEHAVIORS

For those of us whose inner child becomes wounded or forgotten, we may develop self-saboteurs like the judge, the controller, the hyper-achiever, the stickler, the avoider, the hyper-rational, the victim, the hyper-vigilant, the restless, and the pleaser. These behaviors are defense mechanisms that we create to protect our wounds from becoming deeper as we face the brutality of people's actions in the ego-driven world. Unknowingly, we pass these saboteurs on to our children as they learn from us.

The Judge Saboteur

The Judge stands as the most powerful saboteur, constantly scanning for what's wrong—with yourself, others, and circumstances. This relentless fault-finding creates a cascade of painful emotions: disappointment, anger, regret, guilt, shame, and persistent anxiety about what might go wrong next.

What makes the Judge particularly destructive is its ability to activate other saboteur patterns, compounding the negative spiral and amplifying self-defeating thoughts.

The Judge manifests in three ways:

> Self-criticism: You constantly berate yourself, replaying mistakes and inadequacies endlessly. Your inner dialogue becomes harsh and unforgiving.

Criticism of others: You fixate on others' flaws and failures, damaging relationships and preventing genuine connection.

Negative framing: You interpret situations through a lens of what's wrong, what won't work, and why things will fail, completely overlooking opportunities.

The Judge speaks through familiar refrains:

- "What's wrong with me?"
- "What's wrong with them?"
- "What's wrong with this situation?"

These aren't genuine curiosity—they're accusations disguised as inquiries, designed to confirm the Judge's negative worldview.

The Judge generates guilt about actions, regret about choices, shame about identity, and disappointment in performance. When aimed outward, it fuels anger. Underlying all of these is anxiety—constant worry about past mistakes and future failures.

The Judge tells convincing lies:

- "Without me, you'd become lazy and complacent."
- "I help you learn from mistakes."
- "I'm protecting you from getting hurt."
- "Self-criticism drives improvement."

These justifications keep the Judge in power while undermining well-being and effectiveness.

The Judge is the primary source of suffering. It creates significant anxiety and emotional distress, damages relationships by preventing authentic connection, and keeps you stuck in cycles of negativity rather than moving forward with wisdom.

The Judge developed as a survival mechanism. Our ancestors who anticipated dangers and focused on what could go wrong were more likely to survive threats. This negativity bias helped prevent surprise attacks.

However, what served as protection in life-or-death situations now operates constantly in modern life, where most situations don't require this vigilance. The Judge mistakes everyday challenges for existential threats, keeping you in perpetual defensive alertness that no longer serves your well-being.

The Controller Saboteur

The Controller operates from an anxiety-fueled need to maintain control over situations and people. While effective in certain contexts, the Controller's approach often creates unintended consequences that undermine long-term success and relationships.

The Controller is willful, confrontational, and unflinchingly direct. The Controller pushes people beyond their comfort zones and actively seeks challenges, viewing obstacles as invitations to assert dominance.

The Controller connects with others primarily through competition and conflict rather than softer, vulnerable emotions. Their communication style frequently intimidates and can be perceived as anger or harsh criticism.

The Controller is confident, action-oriented, and decisive when others hesitate. This saboteur challenges self and others to achieve ambitious goals and makes tough, unpopular decisions that others avoid. The Controller excels at recognizing possibilities and mobilizing people toward desired outcomes.

The Controller operates from a core belief: "I must control situations and people to ensure the outcomes I need." This generates intense anxiety whenever things don't unfold according to plan.

When others don't comply, anger and intimidation emerge reflexively. The Controller experiences impatience with different emotional styles and often feels hurt by perceived challenges to their authority, though rarely admitting this vulnerability.

The Controller's lies:

- "Without my control, productivity and results will suffer."
- "Pushing people hard is necessary—it's how success happens."
- "If I let go of control, I'll be controlled by others."
- "I'm doing this for the team's benefit."

The Controller may achieve short-term results, but at significant cost. People feel resentful, controlled, and diminished. They comply outwardly while harboring internal resistance, undermining sustained success.

For the Controller, attempting to control inherently uncontrollable aspects generates chronic anxiety. The Controller lives with constant tension, always vigilant for threats, never truly at ease.

The Controller typically develops when control becomes a survival strategy in chaotic, unpredictable, or dangerous environments. Often, the Controller emerges from experiences of hurt, rejection, or betrayal. What began as protection became a limiting pattern.

The Hyper-Achiever Saboteur

The Hyper-Achiever operates from a belief that your worth depends entirely on constant performance and achievement. This saboteur creates dependence on external validation that becomes an exhausting, never-ending cycle. No matter how much you accomplish, it's never enough.

The Hyper-Achiever drives unsustainable workaholic tendencies. Most tragically, this saboteur causes you to lose touch with deeper emotional and relational needs, substituting authentic connection with hollow approval from accomplishments.

Hyper-Achievers are driven, pragmatic, and exceptionally goal-oriented. They possess a remarkable capacity to inspire both themselves and others toward meaningful growth and significant achievements. When this energy becomes inner-directed rather than externally focused, these individuals can accomplish extraordinary things.

The Hyper-Achiever is intensely competitive and acutely conscious of image and status. Hyper-Achievers become skilled at masking insecurities behind a polished, positive facade that projects confidence.

This saboteur is chameleon-like, adapting personality to impress different audiences. The focus remains on cultivating and protecting public image rather than engaging in genuine introspection.

Core beliefs that drive this pattern:

"I need to be the best at everything I do." Mediocrity is intolerable.

"Efficiency and effectiveness are what matter most." Time and energy must be optimized for maximum productivity.

"Emotions are distractions that interfere with performance." Feelings are obstacles to overcome.

"My worth is determined by my success and others' approval." Without achievements and external validation, there is no inherent value.

Hyper-Achievers feel deeply uncomfortable dwelling on feelings, perceiving them as distractions. Beneath the driven exterior, they often experience occasional emptiness and depression, especially in rare quiet moments. Success becomes crucial not just for external recognition but for feeling any sense of worthiness.

Many Hyper-Achievers also harbor a fear of intimacy and vulnerability. True closeness requires revealing the person beneath the achievements—who may feel inadequate without accomplishments to justify their existence.

The Hyper-Achiever's Rationalizations

- "Life is fundamentally about achieving and producing results."
- "Maintaining a good image is essential for achieving results."
- "Feelings are distractions that hinder success."

Happiness becomes fleeting, limited to brief celebrations immediately following achievements—quickly cut short by the drive toward the next goal. There's never time to truly savor success.

Self-acceptance becomes entirely conditional, dependent on ongoing success. One failure can trigger a collapse in self-worth. This conditional self-regard creates constant anxiety.

The emotional disconnection also hinders genuine, deep relationships. Others may admire you, but they don't truly know you.

The Hyper-Achiever develops when love and validation become tied to performance. Self-worth becomes conditioned on achievements and external approval rather than being inherent and unconditional.

The child learns a painful lesson: "I am loved for what I do, not for who I am."

The Stickler Saboteur

The Stickler embodies perfectionism and an excessive need for order, organization, and control. This saboteur operates from the belief that there is one right way—the perfect way—and anything less is unacceptable. The Stickler holds impossibly high ideals, creating a rigid framework that leads to chronic frustration.

The Stickler is methodical, punctual, and remarkably self-disciplined. But when driven by this saboteur, these qualities become sources of constant tension. The Stickler experiences persistent frustration when standards aren't met—whether by themselves or others—and this disappointment prevents genuine satisfaction.

Sticklers bring much-needed organization and order to chaotic situations. They can lead others based on clear principles and well-defined standards, creating structure where there was confusion.

Their self-discipline enables them to maintain consistently high standards. They follow through on commitments and take responsibilities seriously. The Stickler is also direct and discerning, capable of seeing situations clearly without sugarcoating.

The Stickler becomes highly critical—both of themselves and others—leading to resentment and anxiety in relationships. People feel they can never measure up, that nothing they do is ever quite good enough.

The Stickler's need for self-control can result in suppressed anger that simmers beneath the surface. When standards inevitably aren't met—because perfection is impossible—this anger seeks release through irritability, sharp criticism, or cold withdrawal.

The Stickler's rigidity drastically reduces flexibility in dealing with change and accommodating different approaches. There's only one acceptable way, which stifles creativity and collaboration.

The Stickler's mindset is characterized by rigid, absolute thinking:

"If something cannot be done perfectly, it shouldn't be done at all."

"There is a right way and a wrong way to do everything."

"Mistakes are unacceptable failures." They represent personal inadequacy rather than natural aspects of learning.

"Order and perfection equal safety and control."

Living with the Stickler generates constant worry about making mistakes and facing criticism—from others, but especially from the harsh inner critic that never rests.

Sarcasm and self-righteousness often emerge as defense mechanisms against perceived inadequacies. Beneath the critical exterior lies deep insecurity and exhaustion from relentless pressure to be perfect.

The Stickler's Justifications:

- "Perfectionism is a personal obligation—it separates excellence from mediocrity"
- "My high standards lead to better quality and greater order."
- "If I relax my standards, everything will fall apart."
- "Being critical is helpful—it pushes people to be better."

Perhaps the cruelest lie: perfectionism will eventually bring peace of mind. In reality, the Stickler's behavior leads to ongoing anxiety that never resolves.

The rigidity creates ongoing anxiety and frustration that permeates daily life. There's never relief, never "good enough," never permission to simply be satisfied.

For those in a relationship with a Stickler, the experience can be demoralizing. They feel continually criticized, leading to self-doubt, resentment, and eventual resignation.

The Stickler's need for perfection can create a toxic environment, stifling creativity, preventing experimentation, and shutting down collaboration.

The Stickler typically develops in chaotic family environments where creating order felt like the only way to manage overwhelming unpredictability.

Others developed perfectionism while seeking acceptance from demanding, critical parents who communicated that love was conditional on performance. Being the "perfect" child became a survival strategy.

The Avoider Saboteur

The Avoider operates from a belief that peace and harmony must be preserved at all costs—even when that cost is your own growth, authenticity, and effectiveness. This saboteur focuses on the positive and pleasant extremely, systematically avoiding difficult tasks, uncomfortable conversations, and unpleasant conflicts.

The Avoider's version of peace is actually a form of numbness—a refusal to engage with reality when reality becomes uncomfortable. This isn't true peace; it's avoidance masquerading as wisdom.

Avoiders genuinely seek peace and harmony, both within themselves and with others. This isn't superficial—it's a deep orientation toward creating calm, balanced environments.

Avoiders possess an easygoing, even-keeled temperament that can be genuinely soothing. They're flexible and adaptable, able to go with the flow. They also tend to be positive and relatively non-judgmental, offering acceptance that can feel refreshing.

The Avoider consistently avoids conflict and says yes to things you don't actually want to do. The word "no" feels dangerous.

The Avoider downplays the importance of real problems and tries to deflect others who want to address them. "It's not that bad," "Let's not make a big deal," or "Maybe it will just work itself out" become familiar refrains.

When you do need to resist something, the Avoider does so through passive-aggressive means rather than direct communication.

Most insidiously, the Avoider causes you to lose yourself in comforting routines and habits, using them as refuges from discomfort. Procrastination becomes a way of life.

The Avoider's Inner World:

- "This is just too unpleasant. Maybe if I let it go, it will take care of itself."
- "If I deal with this now, I will hurt her feelings. I'd rather not."
- "If I get into conflict with others, I might lose my connection with them."
- "I have found balance. I don't want to mess with it."
- "I'd rather give someone else their way than create a scene."

The Avoider maintains an even-keeled surface, but beneath lies persistent anxiety about what has been avoided. Those unaddressed issues don't actually disappear; they create a low-grade background hum of worry.

The Avoider experiences fear about the hard-won peace being interrupted. Perhaps most significantly, the Avoider creates suppressed anger and resentment. You say yes when you mean no, and all of that builds up internally.

The Avoider's Justifications:

- "You are a good person to spare others' feelings."
- "No good comes out of conflict."
- "It is good to be flexible. Someone needs to be the peacemaker."

By denying conflicts and negativities that genuinely exist, you prevent yourself from actually working with them and potentially turning them into gifts and opportunities.

Feeling numb to pain is fundamentally different from knowing how to harvest the wisdom that pain can offer. The Avoider confuses numbness with peace.

What you avoid doesn't actually go away—it festers. Unaddressed issues grow more complex over time.

Relationships remain superficial through conflict avoidance. You can't have genuine intimacy without the willingness to navigate disagreement together.

Others' trust decreases as they sense when negative information is being withheld.

The Avoider can develop in both happy and difficult childhoods.

In a genuinely happy, protected childhood, you might never have learned the resiliency that comes from dealing with difficult emotions.

In a childhood characterized by high conflict and tension, the Avoider might emerge as you learn to play peacemaker. Being calm and pleasant becomes your survival strategy and eventually your identity.

The Hyper-Rational Saboteur

The Hyper-Rational saboteur operates from a belief that the rational mind is supreme—the only truly reliable tool for navigating life. This saboteur focuses intensely and exclusively on rational processing of everything, including relationships and emotions that inherently transcend pure logic.

To others, the Hyper-Rational can appear cold, distant, and intellectually arrogant. From the inside, this saboteur feels like protection—a refuge of order and clarity. The problem is that this refuge becomes a prison, cutting you off from essential dimensions of human experience.

Hyper-Rationals are capable of remarkable depth of insight and understanding through objective analysis. Their analytical capacity isn't superficial—it's genuinely profound.

They're often highly observant and perceptive, noticing patterns and details others miss. They possess the power of intense mental concentration, able to focus deeply for extended periods.

At their best, Hyper-Rationals can be brilliant explorers and inventors, using their analytical gifts to solve complex problems and generate innovative solutions.

The Hyper-Rational creates an intense and active mind that sometimes comes across as intellectually arrogant or secretive. There's often an air of superiority.

People with a strong Hyper-Rational are intensely private and don't let many people into their deeper feelings. When they do show emotion, it's typically through passion about ideas rather than personal vulnerability.

The Hyper-Rational prefers to watch the "craziness" around them from a distance, analyzing rather than participating in the messy emotional reality of human interaction.

There's also a high penchant for skepticism and debate. The Hyper-Rational questions everything and finds intellectual sparring more engaging than emotional connection.

"The rational mind is where it's at." This is the highest human capacity, superior to all others.

"Feelings are distracting and irrelevant." Emotions cloud judgment; they should be minimized.

"Many people are so irrational and sloppy in their thinking."

"The needs and emotions of others distract me from my projects."

"I need to shut out intrusions."

"What I value most is knowledge, understanding, and insight."

"My self-worth is attached to mastering knowledge and demonstrating competence."

Despite the emphasis on rationality over emotion, the Hyper-Rational generates its own emotional landscape. There's persistent frustration with others for being emotional and "not rational enough."

The Hyper-Rational experiences anxiety about preserving personal time, energy, and resources against intrusions. Every request feels potentially draining.

Beneath the analytical exterior, many Hyper-Rationals feel different, alone, and not understood. The rational mind that feels like such a strength also creates isolation.

There's often underlying skepticism or cynicism.

"The rational mind is the most important thing. It should be protected from the wasteful intrusion of people's messy emotions and needs, so it can get its work done."

This justification sounds logical, even noble. But it's actually a trap that prevents you from developing other essential capacities.

This pattern severely limits the depth and flexibility of relationships by analyzing rather than experiencing feelings. You think about emotions rather than feeling them, study relationships rather than being present in them.

The Hyper-Rational also intimidates people who are less analytically intense. Others may feel judged, inadequate, or dismissed.

Most tragically, the Hyper-Rational prevents you from accessing the wisdom that comes through intuition, empathy, and direct emotional experience. There are dimensions of understanding that simply cannot be reached through analysis alone.

The Hyper-Rational typically develops as a survival strategy in early childhood circumstances characterized by emotional turmoil or chaotic surroundings. When the emotional environment feels overwhelming, unpredictable, or threatening, the rational mind offers refuge.

Escaping into the neat, orderly, rational mind generates a sense of security. For some, intellectual superiority becomes a way to gain attention and praise. Being the smartest person in the room becomes your identity and protection.

The Victim Saboteur

The Victim operates from a belief that emotional pain is both identity and currency—who you are is defined by what you suffer, and suffering is how you earn attention, affection, and validation. This saboteur maintains an extreme and persistent focus on internal feelings, particularly painful ones, creating a dramatic emotional landscape that dominates awareness and relationships.

The Victim is characterized by emotional temperament used strategically, often unconsciously, to gain attention. There's frequently a martyr streak—a sense that you bear burdens others don't understand, that your suffering is both uniquely yours and somehow noble.

These individuals are genuinely sensitive—they feel their own emotions deeply and clearly, including difficult emotions others might avoid. This emotional depth isn't superficial; it's profound.

They're capable of deep and courageous introspection and self-discovery. Victims are individualistic, appreciating the uniqueness of themselves and others in refreshing and authentic ways.

Perhaps most significantly, they're perceptive of the nuanced inner workings of the mind and heart. When channeled through wisdom rather than suffering, this capacity can be used powerfully to connect with others, to teach, to inspire, or to heal.

When criticized or misunderstood, the Victim tends to withdraw, pout, and sulk rather than engaging directly. There's a retreat into emotional isolation that simultaneously signals distress and tests whether others care enough to pursue.

The Victim can be fairly dramatic and temperamental. When things get tough, there's a desire to crumble and give up. "I just can't do this anymore" becomes a familiar refrain.

Beneath the surface, repressed rage simmers—anger that can't be expressed directly results in depression, apathy, and constant fatigue. The Victim becomes unconsciously attached to having difficulties; problems become part of identity rather than temporary challenges.

"No one understands me." You're uniquely misunderstood, isolated in your experience.

"Poor me. Terrible things always happen to me." You're singled out by fate for especially difficult experiences.

"I might be uniquely disadvantaged or flawed."

"I am what I feel." Your identity is entirely defined by your emotional state.

"I wish someone would rescue me from this dreary mess."

The Victim's emotional experience is characterized by persistent dwelling in painful states. You tend to brood over negative feelings for extended periods, replaying hurts long after the initial event.

There's a pervasive sense of feeling alone and lonely, even when surrounded by people you're close to. The emotional isolation feels impenetrable.

Feelings of melancholy and abandonment color daily experience. The Victim also generates envy and engages in negative comparisons.

"Maybe this way I get some of the love and attention that I deserve." Suffering becomes a strategy for extracting care from others.

"Sadness is a noble and sophisticated thing that shows exceptional depth, insight, and sensitivity." Your suffering proves you're more aware, more feeling, more alive than those who seem content.

These justifications transform suffering from a problem to solve into an identity to protect.

Enormous vitality is wasted through constant focus on internal processing and brooding. Energy that could go toward growth, connection, or contribution instead circles endlessly around pain.

Critically, self-pity is a poor substitute for self-love. The Victim seeks sympathy as a replacement for genuine self-acceptance, but sympathy from others never fills the void that only self-compassion can address.

The strategy backfires by pushing people away through constant testing of whether they care enough to stay. Others eventually become exhausted. They feel frustrated, helpless, or guilty that they can't put more than a temporary Band-Aid on the Victim's pain.

The Victim typically develops in response to a childhood experience of not feeling genuinely seen and accepted. When you internalize the message that something is fundamentally wrong with you, emotional distress becomes a strategy to squeeze out affection.

In a painful paradox, the moods and suffering mimic a false sense of aliveness. When you didn't feel noticed for who you were, at least being upset made you feel real and got you noticed.

The Hyper-Vigilant Saboteur

The Hyper-Vigilant saboteur operates from continuous, intense anxiety about all the dangers and everything that could go wrong. This is vigilance that can never rest, never relax, never trust that things might actually be okay. The Hyper-Vigilant lives in constant alertness, scanning the horizon for threats, waiting for the other shoe to drop.

While appropriate vigilance is valuable—even essential—the Hyper-Vigilant takes this strength to an exhausting, counterproductive extreme. The difference between healthy awareness and hyper-vigilance is like the difference between a watchful guard who rests between shifts and one who never sleeps, becoming increasingly ineffective through exhaustion.

These people are genuinely vigilant—they notice risks and dangers others miss. Their sensitivity to potential problems isn't imaginary; they often do identify real issues requiring attention.

Hyper-Vigilants frequently serve as guardians of families, communities, and institutions. They're the ones who think about safety protocols, identify vulnerabilities, and prepare for contingencies. They tend to be loyal, reliable, dependable, and hardworking.

They're capable of genuine perseverance and consistent work toward objectives. They're also often skilled at instituting and preserving systems and structures that impose order and stability.

The Hyper-Vigilant creates a state of being always anxious, with chronic doubts about both self and others. You question your own judgment, your own adequacy, and simultaneously doubt whether others are reliable.

The Hyper-Vigilant develops extraordinary sensitivity to danger signals—the slightest hint of trouble immediately captures attention and triggers alarm. There's a constant expectation of mishap or danger; even when things are going well, you're waiting for something to go wrong.

The Hyper-Vigilant makes you suspicious of what others are up to, operating from the assumption that people make mistakes, drop balls, or have hidden agendas.

To manage the overwhelming sense of threat, the Hyper-Vigilant often seeks reassurance in procedures, rules, authorities, and institutions. External structures feel safer than trusting your own judgment.

"When is the other shoe going to drop?" Things might seem fine now, but disaster is surely lurking.

"If I make a mistake, I fear everyone is going to jump down my throat."

"I want to trust people, but I find myself suspicious of their motives."

"I need to know what the rules are, although I might not always follow them."

The Hyper-Vigilant generates skepticism that often shades into cynicism. Most characteristically, you're often anxious and highly vigilant. The body remains in a state of alert readiness, always prepared for the threat that might emerge at any moment. This chronic activation takes a tremendous toll on physical and mental well-being.

"Life is full of dangers. If I don't look out for them, who will?"

This justification sounds responsible, even noble. But the Hyper-Vigilant confuses appropriate awareness with exhausting constant anxiety, believing that only through unrelenting vigilance can safety be maintained.

Simply put: this is a hard way to live. The constant anxiety burns enormous amounts of vital energy that could otherwise be put to creative, productive, or enjoyable use. You're perpetually exhausted from the effort of constant watchfulness.

Over time, the Hyper-Vigilant loses credibility due to the "crying wolf" phenomenon. When you consistently predict disaster and it doesn't materialize, others begin to discount your warnings—even when you're identifying genuine risks.

Most painfully, others eventually begin to avoid the Hyper-Vigilant. The intensity of that anxious energy is draining to be around.

The Hyper-Vigilant typically develops from early experiences where the sources of safety and security—usually parental figures—were unpredictable and unreliable. When you couldn't count on caregivers to provide stable protection, you learned to become your own vigilant guardian.

The Hyper-Vigilant can also emerge when painful, unexpected events prove that life itself is threatening or unreliable. A sudden loss, trauma, or upheaval teaches the lesson that danger can strike without warning, and the only defense is perpetual watchfulness.

What began as an understandable response to a genuine threat becomes a rigid pattern that persists long after the original danger has passed.

The Pleaser Saboteur

The Pleaser saboteur attempts to gain acceptance and affection indirectly through helping, pleasing, rescuing, or flattering others. While people with this saboteur are naturally empathic, loving, and tuned into others' feelings with potential for high emotional intelligence, they lose sight of their own needs and become resentful as a result.

The Pleaser has a strong need to be liked and attempts to earn this through constant giving. They need frequent reassurance about acceptance and affection, can't express their own needs openly, and instead do so indirectly by making others feel obligated to reciprocate. This can make them come across as needy or too intrusive when trying to help.

Their thought patterns revolve around believing they should put others' needs ahead of their own, feeling bothered when their efforts go unnoticed, and thinking they must rescue others. They feel that expressing their own needs directly is selfish and worry that insisting on those needs will drive others away. Underneath lies resentment for being taken for granted, though they have difficulty expressing it.

The Pleaser justifies this behavior by claiming they help selflessly without expecting anything in return, believing the world would be better if everyone did the same. However, this masks the reality that their giving is conditional and comes with a personal agenda to be liked or loved back—it's ultimately about them, not the other person.

This pattern can jeopardize taking care of one's own needs emotionally, physically, or financially, leading to burnout and resentment. Others may develop dependence rather than learning self-sufficiency, or feel obligated, guilty, or manipulated. The intrusive helping or needy behavior can actually drive people away.

The roots often trace to childhood assumptions: that they must put others' needs first, that asking for their own needs might drive others away, that they must give much love to receive any back, and that they must earn love rather than being inherently worthy of it.

The Restless Saboteur

The Restless Saboteur is constantly in search of greater excitement in the next activity or through constant busyness. Rarely at peace or content with the current activity, restlessness can be a strategy to escape from dealing with fears, anxieties, and painful feelings.

People with the Restless Saboteur bring high energy and vitality to their lives. They're open, curious, spontaneous, with contagious enthusiasm and appreciation of life. They're capable of great productivity, creativity, and breadth of activity, and they can energize and engage others in co-creation.

However, they're easily distracted and can get too scattered. They stay busy juggling many different tasks and plans, seeking excitement and variety over comfort or safety. They bounce (or escape) from unpleasant feelings very quickly, seeking constant new stimulation.

Their thought patterns include: "This isn't fulfilling," "This next thing has got to be more exciting," "These negative feelings suck—I must shift my attention to something exciting," and "Why can't anyone keep up with me?"

They feel impatient with what's happening now, always wondering what's next. There's fear of missing out on other, more worthwhile experiences, restlessness, wanting more and more options, and worry that focusing on any unpleasant feeling will cause it to grow and become overwhelming, and it is best to divert attention instead.

The Restless justifies this by saying life is too short and must be lived fully, that spending time on unpleasant feelings is a waste of life, and attention should be diverted elsewhere.

Underneath the surface of fun and excitement is anxiety-based escape from being present to this moment's full experience, which might include dealing with unpleasant things. The Restless avoids real and lasting focus on issues and relationships that truly matter. Others have difficulty keeping up with the frenzy and chaos, unable to build anything sustainable.

The roots often trace to childhood experiences with inadequate parental nurturing or painful circumstances. Restless indulgence provided substitute self-nurturing and an escape from dealing with anxiety and pain.

Chapter Eight

DIANE'S STORY – A CASE STUDY

Several years ago, a client came to me not knowing how to get the word out about her talent for painting beautiful landscapes. I have seen her work, and it is exceptional! It was especially challenging for her because she knew where to advertise and where to network in the right circles. She had plenty of local contacts, having grown up in the town where she worked and lived. She told no one about her art. Her talent was like a gem hiding in plain sight.

The inability to promote herself also impacted the rest of her life. Not making much money, doing odd house painting jobs here and there, she also suffered from bouts of depression. While part of her inner being was hopeful, the rest felt like she would be stuck forever. She came to me, reluctantly at first, upon the recommendation of a mutual friend.

For the rest of the story, I will refer to my client as Diane, a fictitious name, for my client's desire to remain anonymous.

After having a thorough introductory session, it was clear that Diane had little self-confidence, low self-esteem, a strong case of limiting beliefs, and a strong victim mentality. She refused to believe that she could ever be worthy of being known as a highly talented artist.

Diane believed all the lies she was fed as a child. The reason why I say lies is because, as children, we believe that our lives will be exactly like our parents and other elders tell us life will be. We naturally accept what we are told as irrefutable truth. Our parents do not know any better; they are just doing their best to raise us, as many generations have raised them. They are unknowingly fostering assumptions in their child's mind. These assumptions are imprinted on our brains early in life.

She was the only daughter of a stereotypical middle-class family in the 1950s. Her father was the breadwinner, and her mother stayed home, took care of the house, and nurtured the family. Her father only encouraged her brothers to excel in school, get into a reputable college, and graduate in good standing so they would have the best chance of embarking on a successful career and becoming family men like himself. The thought never crossed her father's mind that Diane desired to be recognized as an equal to her brothers and deserved the same encouragement for her future. His only concern for her was that she met and married an appropriate spouse who would provide for her and the family they would raise together. This was the social norm during those days, so Diane's mother never questioned her husband's intentions for their daughter. The norm was to accept the father's intentions for his children and not question them. Diane took comfort in her art and just accepted what was.

It is not surprising that the children of the 1950s became the establishment-hating generation that came of age in the late 1960s and 1970s, the anti-establishment. Especially for women, the repressed thoughts of gender inequality were slowly bubbling to the surface. Diane became a hippie, left home, and moved in with a friend after high school for about a year. She hung out a lot in Greenwich Village in New York City. Being the dreamer that she was, this was her escape. After all, Greenwich Village was the artsy district where many great artists got their start.

Eventually, moving into her apartment in the same town where she grew up, she was determined to live independently and never took an interest in settling down with a significant other. She had an obvious resentment of her parents, and the relationship between her and them was rocky, to say the least. Diane had several acquaintances and socialized frequently, but only had a few very close friends. She had difficulty respecting relationship boundaries and felt slighted when a friend chose to associate with someone else outside their friend group. Her lack of self-confidence and self-esteem prevented her from stepping out of her comfort zone. She rarely met new people, and when she did, it was due to strong encouragement from a close friend.

Although Diane did not attend college, she was self-educated. She developed a keen knowledge of the great masters, their unique styles, and the historical periods associated with their art, and could converse with art enthusiasts. Still, she felt embarrassed that she did not have a formal art education. She had strong imposter syndrome and avoided getting too deeply involved in these conversations.

When Diane and I first met, she was well into her 40s and had adjusted to her lifestyle, but was not happy and longed to see her dreams of selling her pastoral landscapes become a reality. She was very reluctant to work with me at first. Many people still mistrusted unfamiliar or unconventional methods like life coaching in 2010. The only reason she consented to life coaching was our mutual friend's constant encouragement to at least try it. She kept "nagging," in Diane's words, until she agreed. I am so thankful for our mutual friend because if not for this connection, Diane's life path may never have changed. I believe there are no chance meetings, no coincidences, and there is a reason for everything. I truly believe that I am meant to meet everyone on my life path for the lessons I can learn from them and for the lessons they can learn from me.

Toward the middle of our first session, Diane began to relax into the conversation. She was no longer interjecting jokes or making sarcastic remarks during our conversation. She had her first 'aha moment,' which is a term coaches use to describe a client's sudden realization or epiphany. She realized something that previously never entered her thoughts and began the process of looking at life and herself through a different lens. Diane began to realize that nothing is set in stone, not even her life path. The concept of choice had been rejected previously by her brain, and now she was open to considering that the choice was real.

Soon after, she looked forward to our sessions. At the beginning of each session, she used to say, "What am I going to find out about myself today?" I began to see the transformation of this woman from a shy, sarcastic, insecure, highly talented artist to a more outgoing, unpretentious, confident, highly talented artist. She changed from being fearful, hiding behind others, to a fearless, outgoing person looking to take on the world. As a coach, I experienced a sense of gratitude for being there during her transformation and total fulfillment in knowing that I had chosen to become a life coach.

After one month of working with me, this amazing woman had a big shift. Diane realized that she could self-promote her work to the people who hired her for house painting. Many of her customers were wealthy and art collectors. Before working with me, Diane did not speak much to her customers other than to get the job specifications and collect payment. With her newfound confidence, she felt comfortable making conversation about the paintings hanging on the walls of their houses.

In some instances, she would ask them if they were interested in seeing some samples of her art. She was pleasantly surprised when they accepted her invitation and practically overwhelmed with joy when they commissioned a painting. She began receiving commissions for paintings from people in her community and the surrounding communities. Some of the people in the area were in the same networking circles, and by "word of mouth," she received inquiries about her artwork the same way she received inquiries for house painting. She said she felt like a little kid again and was excited about her future.

She attributes this shift to identifying her limiting beliefs and other self-sabotaging behaviors that were holding her back from putting herself out there. The key to her success was the willingness to have a vision for her growth into the life she was meant to have. Her continuing belief that she can paint her life into the unique vision she has for it is what drives her forward every day.

Now, her life is quite strikingly different. Diane continues to paint custom canvases for local clients and shows her work in galleries and art exhibitions in her local and surrounding communities.

Key Findings Related To Positive Intelligence

Becoming mentally fit involves strengthening good behaviors like empathy, curiosity, creativity, calmness, and clear-headed action to overcome behavioral saboteurs like the judge, hyper-achiever, stickler, avoider, hyper-rational, victim, hyper-vigilant, restless, and pleaser.

Just like we exercise our physical muscles to get fit, we need to overcome our saboteurs through good behavioral practices. We strengthen our mental muscle of self-command to change the neural pathways in our brain to form new behaviors that become permanent habits. This may sound mind-boggling to some people, but it is neuroscience.

If you are experiencing negative emotions, you are in saboteur mode. By assuming what we, as mental fitness trainers, call the sage perspective (good behavior), every problem can be converted into a gift or opportunity.

Diane was judging herself, others, and her situation by making assumptions. Judgment is our master behavioral saboteur, and all the other saboteurs are accomplices. She exhibited the avoider saboteur by keeping her artwork a secret, and she avoided talking about her art. Diane avoided socializing freely with groups of people. She always had to be sure that someone she trusted as a close friend would accompany her. Eventually, as she gained self-confidence, her curiosity overcame this saboteur, and she became more social in unfamiliar groups.

We already know that in Diane's case, she was exhibiting the victim saboteur. Through the sage perspectives of curiosity and creativity, she decided to consider her home painting customers as opportunities (prospects) for her artwork and took clear-headed action to engage with them to pursue her dream.

Diane exhibited the pleaser saboteur. She became excessively attached to whomever she considered a close friend and would do anything for that person to maintain their friendship. Unlike her other acquaintances, who knew nothing about her art, Diane openly shared her art with close friends and gave her art to them as gifts. She was jealous of others who 'invaded' her time with her close friends and openly disrespected the boundaries of these relationships. Out of jealousy, she often made sarcastic remarks about 'the invader' to others in their shared group of friends, and thought she was right in doing so. This behavior disappeared once Diane realized that she could be empathetic towards others. She began to respect boundaries when she let go of the victim mentality.

Chapter Nine

SAGE POWERS – TURNING EVERY CHALLENGE INTO A GIFT

Remember when I told you about Diane, the talented artist who hid her gift from the world, convinced she wasn't good enough? Her transformation didn't happen because I had all the answers. It happened because she learned to shift her perspective, to see herself and her circumstances through what we call the Sage perspective.

This is the heart of mental fitness. And it's where the real magic happens.

Picture this: Something happens in your life. Maybe you lose a job. A relationship ends. A client says no. A dream doesn't pan out the way you imagined.

In that moment, you're standing at a fork in the road.

Down one path, your saboteurs are screaming. "This is BAD! You're not good enough. You'll never succeed. Everything is falling apart." That's your Judge, your Victim, your Avoider—all the saboteurs we've talked about—pulling you into negative emotions, stress, and paralysis.

Down the other path, your Sage is quietly waiting. "This is a GIFT. What can I learn here? How can I grow? What opportunity is hiding in this challenge?"

Here's the truth that changed everything for Diane, and I believe can change everything for you: Whichever perspective you choose becomes your reality.

Your Sage lives in a completely different region of your brain than your saboteurs. While the saboteurs operate from the survival brain, the part that kept our ancestors alive when they faced physical threats, the Sage operates from the region associated with positive emotions, peace and calm, clear-headed focus, creativity, and big-picture thinking.

When you're in Sage mode, you're not reacting from fear or anxiety. You're responding from wisdom and possibility.

The Sage operates from a fundamental belief that might seem counterintuitive at first: Every outcome or circumstance can be turned into a gift and opportunity. Not that everything that happens *is* good, but that everything that happens *can become* something valuable if we choose to see it that way.

This isn't about toxic positivity or pretending bad things don't hurt. It's about recognizing that you have power, the power to choose your response, to find meaning, and to create something new from whatever life hands you.

The Three Gifts Technique

When Diane first came to me, she couldn't see past her circumstances. She was stuck in victim mode, convinced her life would always be limited, that her art would forever remain her "guarded secret." But as she began to shift into the Sage perspective, she discovered what I now teach as the Three Gifts Technique.

This is a practical tool you can use any time you're facing a challenge, setback, or unwanted circumstance. Instead of letting your saboteurs run wild with their catastrophic interpretations, pause and ask yourself three questions:

Gift 1: Knowledge

What knowledge would I need to gain so that the payoff in the future could be much larger than what this is costing me now?

Every difficult situation contains hidden lessons. Maybe you need to learn better boundaries. Maybe you need to understand a new skill. Maybe you need to discover something about yourself that you've been avoiding.

When Diane started asking this question, she realized she needed to learn how to have conversations about her art. She needed to understand that talking about her work wasn't bragging—it was sharing something valuable. She needed to gain knowledge about how successful artists actually build their careers, and it wasn't by hiding.

What knowledge is your current challenge trying to teach you?

Gift 2: Power

Which mental muscle or power must grow to handle this challenge?

Think of your problems as weights in a gym. You don't curse the barbell for being heavy—you recognize that the weight is what makes your muscles grow stronger. The same is true for life's challenges. They're not punishments; they're training equipment for your mind and spirit.

Diane needed to strengthen multiple mental muscles. Her curiosity had to overcome her avoider saboteur. Her self-command had to grow stronger than her victim mentality. Her ability to take clear-headed action had to develop despite her fear of rejection.

See the problem as the resistance against which your mental muscles grow. Ask yourself: What power is this situation requiring me to develop? Empathy? Courage? Resilience? Creativity? Self-command? The ability to intercept your saboteurs?

What's the gift of that power growing? Once you develop it through this challenge, you'll have it for every future situation.

Gift 3: Inspiration

What inspiring action can I commit to that I wouldn't have taken if this "bad" thing hadn't happened?

This is where the rubber meets the road. This is where you take everything you're learning and growing and translate it into concrete action that moves you forward.

For Diane, her gift of inspiration was radical: She decided to start conversations about her art with her house painting customers. She had painted houses for wealthy art collectors for years without ever mentioning her pastoral landscapes. Can you imagine? She was literally surrounded by her ideal clients and had never said a word.

But once she adopted the Sage perspective, once she saw her situation as an opportunity rather than a limitation, she found the courage to act. And that action—born directly from her challenge—became the turning point in her entire career.

That action becomes the gift. Not just the decision, but the doing of it.

The Sage in Action

I want you to understand something important: The Sage perspective isn't about being unrealistically optimistic or pretending everything is easy. Diane's transformation wasn't smooth or instant. She had setbacks. Some customers weren't interested. Some conversations felt awkward. Old saboteurs tried to pull her back into hiding.

But here's what changed: She had learned to pause at the fork in the road. She had practiced choosing the Sage path. And gradually, that choice became more natural, more automatic, more like her default setting.

When she exhibited Level 5 energy—the Opportunist level where "we both win"—she wasn't just thinking about her own success. She was creating value for her clients, too. Her custom paintings brought joy to their homes. Her house painting work supported her art career. Her willingness to be vulnerable and share her gift inspired others to pursue their own dreams.

This is what mental fitness looks like in real life. It's not about never having negative emotions. It's about building the mental muscle to recognize when your saboteurs have hijacked your brain, pause, and consciously choose the Sage perspective instead.

The Five Sage Powers

Your Sage doesn't just offer you a different perspective—it gives you five distinct powers to navigate life's challenges. Think of these as tools in your mental fitness toolkit. Each one serves a specific purpose, and together they form a complete system for responding wisely to whatever life throws your way.

I want you to understand something important: The Sage perspective isn't about being unrealistically optimistic or pretending everything is easy. Diane's transformation wasn't smooth or instant. She had setbacks. Some customers weren't interested. Some conversations felt awkward. Old saboteurs tried to pull her back into hiding.

But here's what changed: She had learned to pause at the fork in the road. She had practiced choosing the Sage path. And gradually, that choice became more natural, more automatic, more like her default setting.

This is what mental fitness looks like in real life. It's not about never having negative emotions. It's about building the mental muscle to recognize when your saboteurs have hijacked your brain, pause, and consciously choose the Sage perspective instead.

Empathize: The Power of Connection

Empathy is your ability to understand and connect with yourself and others without judgment. It's the power that allows you to see beneath the surface, to recognize the humanity in everyone, including yourself.

When you activate empathy, you stop seeing people as obstacles or threats. You see them as complex human beings doing their best with what they know. You also extend that same compassion to yourself—acknowledging your struggles without harsh self-judgment.

Diane struggled with empathy early on. She judged her parents harshly for their 1950s mindset. She resented friends who had other relationships outside their friendship. She couldn't empathize with herself for not having formal art training. But as she developed this Sage power, something beautiful happened. She stopped seeing her customers as just paycheck providers and started seeing them as people who might genuinely appreciate beautiful art. She began respecting boundaries in friendships. She forgave herself for not following a traditional path.

Empathy opens doors that judgment slams shut.

Explore: The Power of Curiosity

Exploration is your power to approach life with fascination and openness. It's the ability to ask "What if?" and "I wonder..." instead of declaring "That's just how it is."

When you explore, you're in discovery mode. You're investigating possibilities rather than defending positions. You're open to learning, experimenting, and being surprised by what you find.

This was the power that helped Diane overcome her avoider saboteur. Instead of assuming her house painting customers wouldn't be interested in her art, she got curious. What if she asked about the paintings on their walls? What if she showed them samples of her work? What if some of them actually wanted to commission a piece?

Curiosity transforms assumptions into experiments. It shifts you from "I already know how this will turn out" to "Let's see what happens."

When you explore, you're not attached to a specific outcome—you're genuinely interested in discovering what's possible.

Innovate: The Power of Creativity

Innovation is your ability to create new solutions, perspectives, and possibilities. It's the power that helps you think outside the box, connect disparate ideas, and generate fresh approaches to old problems.

When you innovate, you're not limited by "the way things have always been done." You're free to imagine something entirely different.

Diane innovated when she realized she could merge her house painting work with her art career. Most people would see these as two separate, unrelated jobs. But through the power of innovation, she saw a creative connection: Her house painting clients were already art appreciators with walls to fill. Why not create a bridge between these two worlds?

Innovation also showed up in how she began to market her work—through organic conversations and word-of-mouth rather than traditional advertising she couldn't afford. She created a path that worked for her unique situation.

This power asks: What creative solution haven't I considered yet? What would happen if I tried something completely different?

Navigate: The Power of Clear-Headed Action

Navigation is your ability to choose the best path forward and take decisive action, even in uncertainty. It's the power of discernment, knowing which direction to move and having the clarity to take that first step.

When you navigate, you're not paralyzed by analysis or frozen by fear. You're calmly assessing your options and moving forward with purpose.

This power was crucial for Diane's transformation. She had to navigate past her fear of rejection, her imposter syndrome, and her habit of hiding. She had to discern which actions would move her forward, starting conversations with customers, showing her work, accepting commissions, and then actually taking those steps.

Navigation isn't about having perfect information or guarantees. It's about trusting yourself to make good decisions and adjust course as needed. It's about taking clear-headed action even when you're scared, because you know it's the right direction.

When you navigate effectively, you're steering your life rather than drifting through it.

Activate: The Power of Purposeful Movement

Activation is your power to take decisive, value-driven action aligned with your deepest purpose. It's the momentum power—the ability to move from thinking and planning into doing and being.

When you activate, you're not just contemplating change or talking about possibilities. You're bringing your intentions to life through concrete action.

Diane was activated when she committed to showing her artwork to customers. She activated when she accepted that first commission. She activated when she continued to put herself out there despite her fear. Each activation built momentum, and that momentum carried her forward into the life she was meant to live.

This power asks: What action will I take right now to honor my authentic purpose? What step, however small, will move me closer to where I want to be?

Activation is the bridge between vision and reality. It's where all the other Sage powers come together and manifest in the world.

Using Your Sage Powers Together

Here's what I want you to understand: These five powers don't operate in isolation. They work together, often simultaneously, to help you navigate life from the Sage perspective.

When Diane started conversations with her customers, she was:

- Empathizing with their appreciation for art.
- Exploring whether they might be interested in her work.
- Innovating a new approach to finding clients.
- Navigating past her fear and imposter syndrome.
- Activating her authentic purpose as an artist.

Your saboteurs will try to block each of these powers. Your Judge will tell you empathy is weakness. Your Hyper-Rational will dismiss curiosity as inefficient. Your Stickler will insist there's only one right way (killing innovation). Your Victim will paralyze your navigation. Your Avoider will prevent activation.

But when you strengthen your mental muscle of self-command, when you practice intercepting those saboteurs and choosing the Sage perspective, these five powers become your natural way of operating.

And that's when everything changes.

Your Sage Is Waiting

Right now, you might be facing your own fork in the road. Maybe you're hiding a talent like Diane did. Maybe you're stuck in a situation that feels limiting. Maybe you're letting your saboteurs tell you stories about why you can't, why you shouldn't, why it's too late or too hard or too risky.

Your Sage is waiting for you on the other side of that pause.

It's waiting with empathy instead of judgment. With curiosity instead of rigid thinking. With creativity instead of limitation. With clarity instead of confusion. With purposeful action instead of paralysis.

The question isn't whether challenges will come. They will. Life guarantees that.

The question is: Which path will you choose when you reach the fork in the road?

Because I truly believe—and I've seen it proven in my own life and in the lives of countless clients—that every outcome or circumstance can be turned into a gift and opportunity. Not because everything that happens is inherently good, but because you have the power to make it so.

Your Sage knows this. It's been trying to tell you all along.

Maybe it's time to listen.

Chapter Ten

TRANSFORMATION, REFLECTION, AND GROWTH WORK FOR ALL SABOTEURS

Transforming the Judge

Recognize the Judge as the master saboteur: The Judge activates and empowers all other saboteurs. Weakening the Judge weakens all saboteur patterns. This makes intercepting the Judge the single most powerful intervention in mental fitness.

Label the Judge immediately: The moment you notice judgment—of yourself, others, or circumstances—simply label it: "That's my Judge." This simple act of recognition creates space between you and the pattern.

Distinguish discernment from judgment: The Sage uses discernment—clear-eyed assessment of what is, without the emotional charge of judgment. Discernment says, "This isn't working well." Judgment says, "This is terrible and shouldn't be happening." Help them feel the difference.

Challenge the Judge's lies: Expose the false promises. The Judge claims it will motivate you to improve, protect you from harm, and help you learn from mistakes. In reality, it generates anxiety that impairs performance, creates the very problems it claims to prevent, and keeps you stuck in repetitive patterns rather than learning.

Practice self-compassion: Treat yourself with the kindness you'd offer a good friend facing similar challenges. Self-compassion is more motivating than self-criticism and far more effective at promoting genuine change.

Use the "10% truth" technique: When the Judge attacks you or others, ask: "What's the 10% truth here?" Acknowledge the kernel of truth, then let go of the 90% exaggeration and distortion. This satisfies the Judge's legitimate concern while releasing its toxic grip.

Intercept the Judge early: The Judge gains power the longer it runs. Catch it in the first few seconds, before it builds momentum and activates other saboteurs. Early interception is the key to mental fitness.

Replace judgment with curiosity: Instead of "What's wrong?" ask "What's interesting here?" or "What can I learn?" This shifts from judgment to exploration, from criticism to growth.

Transforming the Controller

Shift from control to influence: Short-term control often undermines long-term influence. True leadership inspires rather than dominates.

Channel power constructively: Use energy and decisiveness to motivate rather than intimidate, challenge without diminishing.

Expand connection beyond conflict: Genuine connection occurs through collaboration, empathy, and support—not just challenge and debate.

Reframe vulnerability: Vulnerability isn't weakness—it's essential for intimacy, trust, and authentic relationships.

Redirect the challenge inward: Master your mind rather than control external circumstances and people.

Transforming the Hyper-Achiever

Recognize the emptiness: Achievement-oriented fulfillment is inherently hollow. No amount of external success will fill the void created by a lack of self-acceptance.

Reclaim power from external validation: Giving others the power to determine your worth keeps you trapped. True power comes from internal validation.

Cultivate unconditional self-love: Develop emotional awareness as the foundation for accepting and loving yourself regardless of achievements.

Reframe anxiety-inducing challenges: Shift from viewing tasks as tests of worth to seeing them as opportunities for growth and self-actualization.

Distinguish between doing and being: You have value simply by existing, not only by achieving.

Transforming the Stickler

Create the 80/20 framework: Identify which tasks truly require high quality (about 20%) and which can be done "good enough" (the remaining 80%). This distinction frees enormous energy.

Explore the real costs: Encourage honest examination of what their critical nature costs in relationships, peace of mind, joy, and creativity.

Reframe perfection: Help them redefine what perfect order and harmony actually mean. Perhaps true perfection includes flexibility, compassion, and acceptance of imperfection.

Practice imperfection intentionally: Deliberately do things imperfectly as an experiment. Notice that catastrophes rarely materialize.

Develop self-compassion: Treat yourself with the same kindness you might offer a good friend.

Transforming the Avoider

Celebrate the underlying strength: Help them recognize and honor their genuine capacity for creating peace and harmony, so they can release any shame associated with the Avoider pattern.

Distinguish numbness from wisdom: Show them the profound difference between using numbness as a strategy versus accessing the Sage's combination of discernment and action.

Practice feeling difficult emotions: Before shifting to the Sage perspective, help them actually feel their "negative" emotions, including anger.

Reveal how Sage transforms conflict: Demonstrate how the Sage perspective can convert conflicts into gifts—opportunities for growth, deeper connection, and creative solutions.

Practice healthy boundaries: Have them practice saying a healthy "no" to both themselves and others. Start with small, low-stakes situations.

Work with procrastination systematically: Create a procrastination list ordered by importance. After substantial time strengthening Sage perspective, approach with: "What's the highest item on this list I'm willing to tackle now?" Keep moving down until something feels accessible. Don't allow the Judge to create shame about not choosing the top items.

Transforming the Hyper-Rational

Use the toolbox analogy: The hammer of the rational mind is incredibly useful—we're not taking that tool away. We're simply adding more tools so you can choose the right one for each situation.

Reveal the cost in relationships: Help them honestly see the high price they pay in relationships and intimacy. Ask: "Would you rather be right or happy?"

Distinguish appropriate tool use: Help them discern which problems genuinely benefit from data and analysis versus which require empathy, intuition, or other approaches.

Develop empathy as a critical tool: For situations where emotions are engaged—which is most human situations—empathy is essential. Empathizing with someone doesn't mean agreeing with them.

Cultivate intuition for complex problems: Intuition becomes critical for genuinely complex problems. "The rational mind makes you smart. The Sage mind makes you wise."

Show that intimacy requires vulnerability: Real connection cannot be analyzed into existence. It requires the willingness to be seen, to be uncertain, to experience emotions.

Encourage small experiments: Challenge them to go just 10% beyond their comfort zone and be okay with "messy."

Transforming the Victim

Challenge identity fusion with feelings: "You are NOT what you feel." Feelings are experiences you have, not who you are.

Expose the futility of dwelling: "Dwelling in negative emotions and moods does NOT lead to great discovery of the self." Use the hand-on-hot-stove analogy—you don't need to keep it there to know it's hot.

Affirm common humanity: "You are NOT particularly or uniquely flawed. You're just having a human experience." Everyone has pain, everyone has challenges.

Balance uniqueness and oneness: "You are unique, but you're also very commonly human." Explore how you can celebrate your genuine uniqueness without needing to create separateness through suffering.

Expose the self-fulfilling prophecy: Map out the destructive cycle:

- "No one understands me or cares about me." (belief)
- Emotional drama or complaining to get attention. (behavior)
- Interpreting people's actions selectively to confirm they don't care. (filter)
- Or withdrawing to test if anyone cares enough to come after you. (test)
- People eventually become exhausted and abandon you. (result)
- "See, I told you, no one cares." (confirmation)

Ask: "What price are you paying for your Victim proving herself right, over and over again?"

Use reframing tools: "Yes…And…" (finding the 10% the other perspective is right) and Sage Perspective are particularly helpful in breaking through the Victim's negative cycle.

Convert pain into purpose: "What is the gift of your history of incessantly dwelling in your negative emotions? How could you convert that experience into a gift of connecting with, teaching, inspiring, or healing others?"

Redirect the search for self: "The answer to who you are is not in the incessant thinking or negative feeling mind. It is in the no-thinking, knowing mind: the Sage."

Transforming the Hyper-Vigilant

Expose the central lie about security: "Safety and security cannot be found by controlling external circumstances. It's only found within." This is perhaps the most challenging truth for the Hyper-Vigilant to accept. No amount of vigilance can control all variables. True security comes from developing inner resilience and trust in your ability to handle whatever arises.

Create embodied experiences of safety: Use extended practices to help them actually FEEL more safe and secure in their bodies and notice that it's an internal state, not dependent on external circumstances.

Distinguish hyper-vigilance from wise vigilance: Expose the lie that "constantly anxious hyper-vigilance protects you and your loved ones against dangers LESS than peaceful, calm, clear-headed Sage vigilance." Anxiety clouds judgment, slows reaction time, and causes you to miss important information. Calm, centered awareness is actually far more protective.

Use the 3-Gifts technique against fear: When the Hyper-Vigilant imagines catastrophic outcomes, guide them through finding the potential gifts even in feared scenarios. This doesn't mean bad things are good—it means you have the capacity to find meaning and growth even in difficulty.

Create 80-20 distinction: Help them develop two buckets:

- 20%: The risks that genuinely are worthy of Sage vigilance—situations where awareness and preparation genuinely increase safety.
- 80%: All other concerns were that, even if something went wrong, you'd be fine. The 3-Gifts technique would convert any "bad" outcome into opportunities for learning and growth.

This framework allows the Hyper-Vigilant to honor their protective instincts in the areas that truly matter while releasing the exhausting vigilance around countless concerns that don't warrant such intensity.

Practice calibrated trust: Start with small, low-stakes situations where you consciously choose to trust rather than remaining hypervigilant. Notice that most of the time, things work out reasonably well.

For those working with any saboteur pattern, consider these universal practices:

Honest self-assessment: Identify which saboteurs operate most strongly in your life and what their biggest impacts are. Notice how they affect your energy, relationships, effectiveness, and ability to experience peace or joy.

Access Sage wisdom: Consider what your wisest self would counsel you about each saboteur. What would it mean to maintain the underlying strength while releasing the saboteur's grip?

External observation: Identify people who clearly embody each saboteur pattern. Observing patterns in others helps you recognize them more readily in yourself without defensive reactions.

Compassionate engagement: When you encounter someone displaying strong saboteur tendencies, approach them from your Sage strengths rather than matching their saboteur energy. Invite them to celebrate their genuine underlying strengths while exploring what shifting to Sage wisdom might feel like.

Remember the fundamental truth: Every saboteur represents a strength that has been overused, abused, or distorted by anxiety and fear. The goal isn't to eliminate these aspects of yourself—it's to reclaim the strength and allow your Sage to use it wisely rather than letting the saboteur misuse it.

When you learn to recognize your saboteurs, understand their origins, and compassionately redirect their energy toward Sage wisdom, you don't lose anything valuable. Instead, you gain access to your full capacity—your strengths operating through wisdom rather than fear, your gifts expressed through clarity rather than anxiety, your power channeled through love rather than survival.

This is the journey from saboteur to sage—not a rejection of who you are, but a homecoming to who you've always been beneath the protective patterns that once served you but now limit you. Your saboteurs were never your enemies; they were misguided protectors. And your Sage has been waiting patiently all along, ready to guide you home.

Transforming The Pleaser

- Distinguish between Sage giving (unconditional, joy in the act itself) and Pleaser giving (conditional, with a hidden agenda).
- Practice receiving and asking for needs directly.
- Reframe receiving as allowing others the gift of giving.
- Develop unconditional self-love through Empathize Power.
- Build fierce self-care and boundaries through Activate Power.
- Learn to say "no," recognizing that any "no" is a "yes" to something else.

Here's the thing about the Pleaser: on the surface, it looks like pure generosity. You're the person who always shows up, who helps everyone, who makes sure everyone else is okay. You're empathic, loving, and tuned into everyone's feelings. Sounds pretty good, right?

But here's what's really happening underneath: you're not just giving—you're trading. You're helping because you need to be liked. You're rescuing because you need reassurance. You're flattering because you need affection back. And when it doesn't come? That resentment builds up fast.

The Pleaser tells you that expressing your own needs directly is selfish. If you ask for what you need, people will leave. So you give and give and give, hoping people will notice, hoping they'll feel obligated to reciprocate, hoping you'll finally feel loved.

The justification lie is beautiful: "I don't do this for myself. I help others selflessly. The world would be better if everyone did the same." But watch what happens when someone doesn't appreciate your help or doesn't give back. That's when you realize there was always a price tag attached.

This pattern can wreck you. You burn out. You become resentful. Others either become dependent on your rescuing or they feel manipulated and pull away. Either way, you're not getting what you actually need: genuine connection and love.

The coaching shift is profound: Learn to tell the difference between Sage giving and Pleaser giving. Sage giving is unconditional—the joy is in the giving itself, no return required. Pleasure giving always comes with strings attached.

Practice receiving. Ask for what you need directly. If that feels selfish, remember: you can't pour from an empty cup. When you allow others to give to you, you're actually giving them the gift of feeling generous.

The real work? Developing unconditional self-love. The Pleaser's way of filling the void of feeling unloved will never work. The only solution is learning to love yourself fiercely, set boundaries, and recognize that any "no" to someone else is a "yes" to yourself.

Transforming The Restless

- When feeling restless, STOP and do PQ Reps (physical sensation exercises).
- When feeling negative emotions, STOP—don't use busyness as a distraction.
- Acknowledge feelings and feel them in your body.
- Do PQ Reps on the sensations of emotions.
- Become fascinated with the ordinary through sensory awareness.
- Reconsider multitasking—research shows it's far less efficient than single-tasking.

- Learn that constantly focusing on what's next prevents you from experiencing what is.

The Restless Saboteur looks like someone who's really living life to the fullest. You've got that incredible energy, enthusiasm, and spontaneity. You're always doing something interesting, exploring something new. You're the person everyone wants at the party because you bring that contagious vitality.

But here's what's actually going on: you're running. You're not seeking excitement, you're escaping discomfort. Every time an unpleasant feeling shows up, every time something feels even slightly boring or painful, you bounce to the next thing. You're not living fully; you're avoiding deeply.

The Restless whispers: "This isn't fulfilling. The next thing will be better. Don't sit with these negative feelings – shift your attention to something exciting. Life is too short to waste on unpleasant emotions."

So you stay busy. You juggle multiple tasks. You're always planning the next adventure. You multitask constantly. And anyone who can't keep up with your pace feels like they're holding you back.

But underneath all that fun and excitement is anxiety. You're not comfortable being still. You can't sit with difficult emotions. You're scared that if you stop and feel your feelings, they'll overwhelm you. So you keep moving, keep stimulating, keep escaping.

The impact? You never actually deal with what matters. Your relationships stay surface-level because you won't be present long enough to go deep. You can't build anything sustainable because you're onto the next thing before anything takes root. Others struggle to keep up with your chaos.

Here's the coaching truth: When you feel restless, that's exactly when you need to STOP. Do PQ Reps—sensory exercises that bring you into your body, into this moment. When negative emotions arise, that's your cue to stop running and actually feel them in your body.

The research on multitasking is clear: you're not being efficient; you're being scattered. Single-tasking is far more effective. And those ordinary moments you're skipping past to get to the exciting ones? There's magic there if you'd stop long enough to notice.

The deepest work is learning that the ordinary can be fascinating. The sensation of water on your skin in the shower. The sounds around you. The taste of your food. The feelings in your body—even the uncomfortable ones. When you learn to be present to what is, you stop needing to constantly chase what's next.

Reflection and Growth Work for All Saboteurs

For those working with any saboteur pattern, consider these universal practices:

Honest self-assessment: Identify which saboteurs operate most strongly in your life and what their biggest impacts are. Notice how they affect your energy, relationships, effectiveness, and ability to experience peace or joy.

Access Sage wisdom: Consider what your wisest self would counsel you about each saboteur. What would it mean to maintain the underlying strength while releasing the saboteur's grip?

External observation: Identify people who clearly embody each saboteur pattern. Observing patterns in others helps you recognize them more readily in yourself without defensive reactions.

Compassionate engagement: When you encounter someone displaying strong saboteur tendencies, approach them from your Sage strengths rather than matching their saboteur energy. Invite them to celebrate their genuine underlying strengths while exploring what shifting to Sage wisdom might feel like.

Remember the fundamental truth: Every saboteur represents a strength that has been overused, abused, or distorted by anxiety and fear. The goal isn't to eliminate these aspects of yourself—it's to reclaim the strength and allow your Sage to use it wisely rather than letting the saboteur misuse it.

When you learn to recognize your saboteurs, understand their origins, and compassionately redirect their energy toward Sage wisdom, you don't lose anything valuable. Instead, you gain access to your full capacity—your strengths operating through wisdom rather than fear, your gifts expressed through clarity rather than anxiety, your power channeled through love rather than survival.

This is the journey from saboteur to sage—not a rejection of who you are, but a homecoming to who you've always been beneath the protective patterns that once served you but now limit you. Your saboteurs were never your enemies; they were misguided protectors. And your Sage has been waiting patiently all along, ready to guide you home.

As you think about applying the Sage perspective to your own life, consider these questions:

- What challenge are you currently facing that feels like "bad news"?

- What would change if you saw this challenge as a gift waiting to be unwrapped?
- Using the Three Gifts Technique:
    - What knowledge might this situation be offering you?
    - What mental muscle needs to grow to handle this effectively?
    - What inspiring action could you take that you wouldn't have considered before?

Remember, your saboteurs will judge these questions, mock them, or try to convince you they won't work. That's what saboteurs do. But your Sage is curious, open, and ready to explore.

Which voice will you listen to today?

PART THREE

The Unstoppable You

Chapter Eleven

PATHWAY TO PURPOSE

What are you doing about the things that matter most in your life?

What would you say if you were my new client and I asked you this question? First, you might start naming all the people you cherish most and what you were doing to ensure their lives were as comfortable as possible. Most likely, you would talk about the material things you provide for yourself and your loved ones, and how you were striving for your next promotion to provide even more.

I would stop you right there, and remind you that I asked about the things that mattered most, not the people that matter most, and that I am not talking about material things that make your life more comfortable. You see, I am talking about the 'things' that lead to self-actualization, the things that are necessary to you as an individual to be the person that aligns with your authenticity.

Now, you may be saying, 'What the heck is she talking about?' A lot of people will at first.

Definition of self-actualization: "the process of establishing oneself as a whole person, able to develop one's abilities and to understand oneself", *Collins English Dictionary – Complete and Unabridged, 12th Edition 2014*

After some pondering on the meaning of self-actualization and realizing what I mean by the things that matter most in your life, you will see where I am going here. At the same time, you may or may not care to reach self-actualization. If you do, however, a good place to start is to examine your moral values, and based on what you believe in, you can decide, or at least begin to think about your purpose in life.

If you already understand and agree that self-actualization is important in your life, let this be a reminder to work on the things that matter most.

If you feel like you want to be more and you are searching for your true purpose or calling, do some soul searching to answer some of these nagging questions in your mind.

How many of you can say that you are being who you truly want to be? You love your profession. You love your relationships. You love everything about your life.

Is that true?

Is your life the way you dreamed it would be as a child?

Or are you living the way everyone around you expects you to live, and you have given up your dreams?

Who is the person you truly want to become?

What is it about yourself that you truly already love and want to stay that way?

If you still have your childhood dreams, why not pursue them on the side?

Bring more fulfillment and joy into your life.

Who knows?

You may end up doing whatever it is you enjoy full-time after all. Wouldn't that be great?

Be mindful, though. Purpose is not your profession. It's more like your mission in life.

Explore being creative. What are some hobbies or activities you're considering trying?

Explore them now and share your creations with others.

Some people delay exploring new experiences until retirement. And why do they do that?

The excuses include: they have no time, it costs too much money. But these are all assumptions.

How can you free up time to do more of the things you truly enjoy?

Have fun more often. Think of the things, people, and experiences that light you up. These thoughts automatically put a smile on your face.

We so easily forget what truly makes us happy.

You may wonder why you've forgotten what truly makes you happy, which is so very important.

We forget because many of us have been indoctrinated to believe that it's selfish to do things simply because they make us happy.

Make your bucket list and don't wait. Start doing these things now.

Here's a story, my parents' story.

My parents wanted to save up all their money and wait till they retire, buy an RV, and go traveling all over the country. But unfortunately, my dad passed away before he ever retired. So, all their dreams went up in smoke.

Pick one or two or more items each year of your items on your bucket list and do them.

What's going to make you happy now? Do it now. Live more in the moment.

Stop being such a people pleaser. Stop making others happy at the expense of your happiness.

It can be very fulfilling to be kind and do things for others, but when it starts to impinge on your happiness, stop.

For example, maybe you chose your profession or honored a tradition to make your parents happy, but you hate your job, or you're tired of the traditions.

So, stop them.

Following your heart instead of doing what others want you to do can truly be a way to find your purpose.

Get a journal. Start journaling about the things you love.

Write down your dreams and hopes for your future.

When you accomplish something on your bucket list, write about it.

Keep writing, and you'll be surprised what you can grow from a simple idea.

Final words:

Your pathway to your purpose isn't complicated.

You just have to think from a different perspective.

It's not what you do that constitutes fulfillment.

It's whatever you do, you do it because you love it.

Are you on the right path to where you want to go?

Chapter Twelve

Breaking Free from Procrastination – When Your Avoider Saboteur Takes Control

Procrastination is one of the biggest dream killers I've ever witnessed in my coaching practice.

I've sat across from countless talented, intelligent, capable women who know exactly what they need to do but somehow can't bring themselves to do it. They have brilliant ideas gathering dust. Dreams deferred year after year. Goals written in journals that never see the light of day.

If this sounds familiar, I want you to know something: You're not lazy. You're not undisciplined. You're not broken.

You're being sabotaged.

Remember Diane from earlier chapters? The talented artist who kept her gift hidden for decades? Procrastination was at the heart of her paralysis. But here's what she didn't realize until we worked together: Her procrastination wasn't a character flaw. It was her Avoider saboteur running the show.

The Avoider is one of the most insidious behavioral saboteurs because it disguises itself as perfectly reasonable behavior. It tells you you're being "realistic" or "careful" or "waiting for the right time." Meanwhile, years pass, and nothing changes.

Diane avoided talking about her art. She avoided networking. She avoided putting herself out there. And every day she didn't take action, her Judge saboteur used that as evidence that she really wasn't good enough, which made her avoid even more. It's a vicious cycle that keeps you stuck in place while life passes you by.

The Avoider shows up in many forms:

"I'll start when I have more time."

"I need to learn more first."

"I'm waiting for the perfect moment"

"I don't want to do it wrong."

"What if I fail?"

Sound familiar?

We are so inundated with choice and opportunity that you might even say we are spoiled by having too many choices. There is just so much that we could do, we often fall into overwhelm and end up not doing anything.

Here's the painful truth: With so many demands on your attention, it is becoming ever more difficult to stay focused and act on your best choices. The way you use your time will determine what you create or fail to create for your life.

One of the most destructive effects of procrastination is that it makes you feel out of control. When you don't know what you want, it's all too easy to jump from one task to the next, staying busy but never actually moving forward. You're spinning your wheels, and deep down, you know it.

Diane felt this acutely. She was "busy" with house painting jobs, socializing with close friends, and keeping herself occupied. But she wasn't building the life she truly wanted. She was avoiding it.

And that avoidance cost her decades.

Think about what procrastination might be costing you right now. Not just in terms of goals unmet, but in terms of who you're not becoming, the impact you're not making, the fulfillment you're not experiencing.

If you're experiencing the negative emotions that come with procrastination—anxiety, guilt, shame, frustration—you are in saboteur mode. Your brain is hijacked, and you're reacting from fear rather than responding from wisdom.

The Avoider saboteur is often working alongside other saboteurs:

The Judge tells you that you're not good enough yet, that your work won't be perfect, that people will criticize you. So you wait.

The Hyper-Vigilant scans for everything that could go wrong, making you anxious about taking action. So you freeze.

The Victim convinces you that circumstances are against you, that you don't have what you need, that it's not your fault. So you stay stuck.

The Stickler insists everything must be done perfectly, in the right order, according to the rules. So you never feel ready.

The Restless gets bored easily and jumps to the next shiny thing before completing what you started. So nothing gets finished.

For Diane, her Avoider worked primarily with her Judge and her Victim. She judged herself as not having formal training (therefore not "real" artist material), and she felt victimized by her upbringing and circumstances. These saboteurs formed a powerful alliance that kept her paralyzed for decades.

The Sage Solution: Five Powers Against Procrastination

Having a strategy for overcoming procrastination is critical if you truly want to push past short-term obstacles to create a life of fulfillment. And that strategy starts with activating your Sage powers to counter your saboteurs.

Empathize: Understanding Your Resistance

The first step isn't to beat yourself up for procrastinating. That's just your Judge Saboteur piling on, making things worse. Instead, activate your power of empathy and get curious about what's really going on.

What are you actually afraid of? What is your Avoider trying to protect you from?

For most people, procrastination isn't about the task itself—it's about what the task represents. Fear of judgment. Fear of failure. Fear of success and the changes it might bring. Fear of discovering you're not as capable as you hoped.

When Diane finally empathized with herself, she realized her avoidance was trying to protect her from the pain of rejection. Her inner child had been told she wasn't good enough, and procrastination was a shield against proving that belief true.

Empathy creates space for honest self-examination without harsh judgment. From that space, change becomes possible.

Explore: Getting Clear on What You Really Want

The first strategic step in overcoming procrastination is to get clear on what exactly you want from every area of your life. This clarity will give you the power to look past distractions that may throw you off course. It gives you a direction and a target, which will help you build a vision for your life.

But here's where your Explore power comes in: You need to get curious about not just what you want, but why you want it.

Apart from knowing what you want, you should also develop some strong reasons why you want it. This will give you a sense of purpose and motivation that is critical for staying focused long-term.

Diane had to explore her true desires. Did she want to be a famous artist? Did she want financial success? What she discovered was deeper: She wanted to share beauty with the world. She wanted to be seen and valued for her authentic gift. She wanted to live fully rather than hiding.

When you're clear on your why, procrastination loses much of its power. The pull of your purpose becomes stronger than the push of your fear.

Innovate: Breaking Down the Overwhelming

One of the most powerful strategies for overcoming procrastination is to learn how to break your tasks up into bite-sized pieces. Any task, no matter how big, can be broken down into small, manageable tasks that are easy to do.

This is where your innovative power shines. You're not just following a prescribed path—you're creatively chunking down your "big" tasks in a way that works for you. You're cutting overwhelming goals down to your size.

Diane didn't wake up one day and become a successful artist showing in galleries. That would have been overwhelming. Instead, she innovated small, manageable steps:

First, just mention art in conversation.

Then, show one sample piece.

Then, accept one small commission.

Then, display work in one local venue.

Each step was doable. Each success built confidence for the next step.

What overwhelming goal are you avoiding right now? How could you innovate a way to break it into pieces so small that your Avoider can't use size as an excuse anymore?

Navigate: The Power of Immediacy

One of the quickest ways to overcome procrastination is to learn and utilize the power of immediacy. What can you do immediately? What action can you take right now that will move you closer to your goal?

This is your Navigate power in action—choosing the next right step and taking it.

Doing something, no matter how small, will immediately break your mental pattern of procrastination and put you back in control. Taking the first step, even if it is small, will create momentum, and you will almost automatically be driven to take another step.

Don't wait for everything to be perfect before you take the first step. Just do it. Just get it going. Often, you will only know what to do next after taking that first step.

Diane didn't wait until she felt confident. She didn't wait until she had a portfolio website or business cards, or a perfect elevator pitch. She started a conversation about art with the very next customer. That immediate action created momentum that carried her forward.

What immediate action could you take in the next ten minutes? Not tomorrow. Not when conditions are perfect. Right now.

Activate: From Knowing to Doing

Here's where everything comes together. You can understand your saboteurs. You can know all the strategies. You can have perfect clarity on what you want and why. But none of it matters until you activate—until you actually move.

Activation is the bridge between intention and reality. It's where you stop thinking about your life and start living it.

There simply isn't enough time to do everything, but there is always enough time for the most important things in your life. Success at anything in life requires an investment of time and effort from you. You need to focus and concentrate on creating the desired result.

When Diane activated her authentic purpose as an artist, she stopped letting circumstances control her. She took back her power. She made a choice and committed to it through action.

Like any skill, you need to learn and practice activation until you get good at it. Eventually, it will become an automatic response, and you will develop the habit of taking action despite your fears and apparent limitations.

The Fork in the Road

Every time you face a task you've been avoiding, you're standing at that fork in the road we talked about in the Sage Powers chapter.

Down one path, your saboteurs are offering you comfortable excuses. "Not today. You're too tired. You don't have everything you need. Wait until conditions are better." That path feels safe in the moment, but it leads to regret, stagnation, and the slow death of your dreams.

Down the other path, your Sage is quietly inviting you to take one small step. Just one. Not the whole journey, just the next step. That path might feel scary, but it leads to growth, momentum, and the life you're meant to live.

Which path will you choose?

I want you to remember something important: There are many strategies and skills you can use to overcome procrastination. You don't have to be stuck or spinning your wheels.

Diane spent decades procrastinating before she finally broke free. But when she did, everything changed. Not because she became a different person, but because she learned to recognize her saboteurs, activate her Sage powers, and take action despite her fear.

You can do the same.

Your Avoider saboteur wants you to believe that "someday" you'll be ready. "Someday," you'll have more time, more knowledge, more confidence, more resources.

But your Sage knows the truth: Someday is today. Right now. This moment.

The question is: What will you do with it?

Reflection Questions

Which saboteurs show up most frequently when you procrastinate?

What have you been avoiding that really matters to you? What is that avoidance costing you?

What are you actually afraid will happen if you take action?

If you could take just one immediate step right now, something small and manageable, what would it be?

What knowledge, power, or inspiration might be waiting for you on the other side of your procrastination?

Remember: Your saboteurs will tell you that answering these questions isn't urgent, that you can do it later. That's them talking.

Your Sage is inviting you to pause, reflect, and take one small step forward. Right now.

Which voice will you listen to?

Chapter Thirteen

THE DAILY PRACTICE OF MINDFULNESS – STRENGTHENING YOUR MENTAL FITNESS MUSCLE

If you do not practice mindfulness daily, are you curious about mindfulness?

I ask because mindfulness is not just another self-help trend or wellness buzzword. It's the foundation of mental fitness. It's the practice that makes everything else we've talked about—recognizing your saboteurs, activating your Sage powers, choosing the right path at the fork in the road- possible in real time.

Without mindfulness, you're operating on autopilot. Your saboteurs run the show, and you don't even realize it until you're already deep in negative emotions and reactive behaviors.

With mindfulness, you create space. Space to pause. Space to choose. Space to respond from your Sage instead of reacting from your saboteurs.

Let me tell you a story that illustrates exactly what I mean.

A friend of mine came to me several years ago, visibly exhausted. Her daughter was leaving for college, and she hadn't slept properly in weeks. She was worried sick, worried about her daughter going to a strange place, being with strangers, making good choices, staying safe. The anxiety was consuming her.

"Well, you had daughters who lived away at college," she said to me. "You know what it's like. Weren't you worried sick at first?"

She spoke as if it was normal to lose sleep and worry, as if this level of anxiety was an expected, unavoidable part of life. In her mind, being a good mother meant suffering through sleepless nights and constant fear.

When I told her she didn't have to feel that way, she was shocked. "What do you mean? That's life, and we have to deal with it the best we can."

I agreed with her last point. "Deal the best we can," I said, "but you needn't be worried or anxious."

She looked at me like I had two heads.

Here's what I explained to her, and what I want you to understand: She could choose how she was going to 'be' in this situation. The circumstances were real; her daughter was indeed leaving for college. But her response to those circumstances? That was a choice.

This is where mindfulness becomes not just helpful, but essential.

The key to mindfulness is learning how to be in the present moment. Not the imagined future where terrible things might happen to your daughter. Not the remembered past where you felt safe when everyone was under one roof. The present moment. Right here. Right now.

In our Western culture, it's become almost impossible to focus only on the given moment. Our minds race constantly—planning, worrying, replaying, analyzing, judging. We're everywhere except where we actually are.

Mindfulness is a way to create a balance between the present moment, the past, and the future. It trains you to recognize when your saboteurs have pulled you out of the present and into anxiety about what might happen or rumination about what did happen.

Remember Diane, the artist who hid her talent for decades? Part of her transformation involved developing a mindfulness practice. She had to learn to be present with uncomfortable emotions, fear of rejection, anxiety about showing her work, and excitement mixed with terror when someone commissioned a painting. Before mindfulness, she would have let her Avoider saboteur sweep her away from those feelings and back into hiding.

With mindfulness, she could stay present, feel the emotions, and still take action.

That's the power of this practice.

The Five Components of Mindfulness

Mindfulness isn't one thing—it's a practice built on five essential components. Understanding each component helps you develop a daily practice that actually strengthens your mental fitness muscle.

Component 1: Attention

The first component of mindfulness is attention. Mindfulness is about training your attention, focusing on the present moment and nothing else.

This is harder than it sounds. Your mind wants to wander. Your Restless saboteur gets bored. Your Hyper-Vigilant saboteur scans for threats. Your Controller saboteur wants to plan and strategize.

But when you practice focusing your attention—on your breath, on physical sensations, on what's happening right now—you're literally rewiring your brain. You're strengthening the neural pathways in your Sage brain and weakening the automatic patterns in your saboteur brain.

Mindfulness has been proven to help people with chronic pain who cannot be helped in any other way. Why? When you can train your attention to stay present rather than catastrophizing about the pain, the experience of pain itself changes.

The same is true for anxiety, stress, and the emotional pain your saboteurs create. When you can keep your attention in the present moment, those saboteurs lose their power.

Component 2: Awareness

The second component is awareness. While attention is about where you focus, awareness is about what you notice without judgment.

An example of this awareness in action is becoming aware of how we automatically judge everyone and everything around us. We constantly look through a lens of judgment at everyone and everything. It's our Judge Saboteur's default setting, and most of us don't even realize we're doing it.

"She shouldn't have said that." "He's doing it wrong." "This traffic is terrible." "I'm so stupid for making that mistake." "Why can't they just get it together?"

Judgment. Judgment. Judgment. All day long.

Mindfulness helps us let go of that knee-jerk reaction of judgment and putting labels on everyone and everything. Instead, we connect to reality in a more open and non-judgmental way. We observe what is, rather than immediately categorizing it as good or bad, right or wrong.

This is where your Empathize power gets stronger. When you're aware without judgment, you can see yourself and others with compassion rather than criticism.

For my friend worrying about her daughter, awareness meant noticing her judgments: "I'm a bad mother if I'm not worried." "Something terrible will definitely happen." "I can't handle this." Once she became aware of these judgments, she could question them instead of accepting them as truth.

Component 3: Acceptance

The third component of mindfulness is acceptance, and this is often the toughest one for people to understand and practice.

Acceptance doesn't mean you approve of everything that happens. It doesn't mean you become passive or stop working to change difficult circumstances. And I am definitely not saying to accept false accusations or statements that aren't true from someone.

What I am saying is this: Accept the emotion that comes from that accusation or statement.

Here's what I mean. When someone says something hurtful or untrue about you, you don't have to accept their words as valid. But if you feel anger, hurt, or fear in response—those emotions are real and present. Acceptance means you allow yourself to stay in the moment and feel those emotions rather than fight them or run away from them.

This is hard. I know because I still struggle with it myself.

As a child, I was told that it was wrong to feel anger, and sometimes I still have trouble accepting the feeling of anger when it arises. My Stickler saboteur tells me I "shouldn't" feel that way. My Pleaser saboteur tells me nice people don't get angry. My Judge saboteur uses my anger as evidence that I'm flawed.

But here's the truth: The anger is there whether I accept it or not. Fighting it only makes it stronger and keeps me stuck. Accepting it, allowing it to be present without judgment, lets it move through me and eventually release.

This is where your Navigate power comes in. When you can accept what is, including difficult emotions, you can make clearer decisions about how to move forward.

Diane had to accept her fear of rejection. Do not give in to it, but accept that it was present. Once she stopped fighting the fear and trying to make it go away before she took action, she could act despite the fear.

That's the gift of acceptance.

Component 4: Non-Identification

The next component of mindfulness is non-identification, and this one can be genuinely life-changing when you understand it.

This component of mindfulness helps us not to react to anger or fear, or any emotion. It teaches us this essential truth: We are not the emotions we feel. We are not the thoughts that emerge.

Think about that for a moment.

When somebody says, "I am sad," that's not actually true. The truth is "I am experiencing sadness." There's a profound difference.

When you say "I am sad," you identify with the emotion. You become it. It defines you. It takes over your entire sense of self.

When you say "I am experiencing sadness," you create distance. You become the observer of the emotion rather than the emotion itself. You can watch sadness move through you like weather moving through the sky. The sky doesn't become the storm—it simply holds space for the storm to pass.

This is what mindfulness teaches us to do. We observe our emotions, our thoughts, our saboteurs, without becoming them.

"I notice my Judge saboteur is criticizing me right now." "I'm experiencing anxiety about this presentation." "My Victim Saboteur is telling me I'm powerless."

When you can observe without identifying, you have space to choose differently. You activate your power of Exploration, getting curious about what's happening without being swept away by it.

My friend with the daughter who is going to college? Once she learned non-identification, she could notice: "I'm experiencing anxiety about my daughter's safety" instead of "I am a terrified wreck who can't function." That distinction changed everything.

Component 5: Choice

Finally, we arrive at the component that brings everything together: choice.

We can choose how to 'respond' rather than 'react'. We are changing our pattern of behavior. We are choosing, we are making a conscious choice.

This is your Activate power in its purest form.

Without mindfulness, you're on autopilot. Something happens, your saboteurs react, and you're swept along in behaviors you didn't consciously choose. You snap at your partner. You avoid an important conversation. You eat a pint of ice cream. You scroll social media for hours. You don't even realize you're making choices; you just react.

With mindfulness, something happens. You pause. You notice your saboteurs activating. You feel the emotion without identifying with it. You consider your options. And then you choose, consciously, deliberately, how you want to respond.

This is mental fitness in action. This is what we've been building toward in every chapter of this book.

Diane practiced this every single time she felt the urge to hide her artwork. The impulse would arise (stimulus), she would pause, notice her Avoider and Judge saboteurs, feel the fear without letting it control her, and then choose to show her work anyway (response).

Each time she did this, she strengthened her mental fitness muscle. Each time, the choice became a little easier. Each time, she proved to herself that she could handle whatever happened.

That's what a daily mindfulness practice gives you: the ability to choose your life instead of just reacting to it.

Making Mindfulness a Daily Practice

Here's what I want you to understand: Mindfulness isn't something you do once and check off your list. It's not a weekend retreat or an occasional meditation when you're stressed.

Mindfulness is a daily practice that strengthens your mental fitness muscle the same way physical exercise strengthens your body.

Just like you wouldn't expect to get physically fit by working out once a month, you can't expect to build mental fitness without consistent daily practice.

The good news? You don't need hours. Even a few minutes a day, practiced consistently, will begin to rewire your brain and strengthen your Sage powers.

Here are some ways to integrate mindfulness into your daily life:

Start your day with mindful breathing. Before you check your phone, before you jump into your to-do list, spend just two minutes focusing on your breath. Notice the sensation of air entering and leaving your body. When your mind wanders (and it will), gently bring your attention back to your breath.

Practice PQ reps throughout the day. These are brief 10-second exercises where you bring your full attention to physical sensations—the feeling of your feet on the floor, the texture of something you're touching, the sounds around you. These micro-practices interrupt saboteur patterns and strengthen your Sage brain.

Create mindful transitions. When you move from one activity to another, from work to home, from one meeting to the next, take a moment to pause, breathe, and reset. This prevents you from carrying stress and sabotaging energy from one situation into the next.

Notice your judgments without judgment. Throughout the day, become aware when your Judge saboteur is labeling and categorizing. Don't beat yourself up for judging (that's just more judging). Simply notice it and get curious about it.

Feel your emotions fully. When emotions arise, resist the urge to push them away or distract yourself. Take a few moments to actually feel them in your body. Where do you notice the emotion? What sensations come with it? This builds your capacity to accept and move through emotions rather than being controlled by them.

The key is consistency. Daily practice, even in small doses, creates lasting change.

Mindfulness and Your Saboteurs

Each of your saboteurs will try to interfere with your mindfulness practice. Knowing this in advance helps you recognize and intercept them:

Your **Judge** will tell you you're doing it wrong, that you're not good at meditation, that this isn't working.

Your **Avoider** will help you find excuses to skip your practice, too busy, too tired, and can start tomorrow.

Your **Restless** will get bored and want to quit after two minutes.

Your **Hyper-Achiever** will turn mindfulness into another performance metric, another thing you have to excel at.

Your **Stickler** will insist you must do it perfectly, for exactly the right amount of time, in exactly the right way.

Your **Victim** will convince you that mindfulness works for other people but won't work for you.

See them coming. Name them when they show up. And practice anyway.

That's the practice within the practice.

The Life You Can Create

I hope I have given you some food for thought about why mindfulness matters and how it works.

My friend with the daughter who is going to college? She started a daily mindfulness practice. Within two weeks, she was sleeping better. Within a month, she was actually excited about her daughter's new adventure instead of being paralyzed by fear. She still cared deeply, still checked in regularly, still had concerns like any parent would. But she wasn't consumed by anxiety. She had learned to be present with her actual life instead of being lost in catastrophic imaginings.

That's what mindfulness gives you: your life back.

Diane's transformation wasn't just about learning to promote her artwork. It was about learning to be present with fear, discomfort, and uncertainty without letting those feelings control her choices. Her daily mindfulness practice made everything else possible.

When you practice mindfulness daily, you're not just feeling calmer or less stressed (though that happens too). You're fundamentally changing your relationship with your thoughts, emotions, and life experiences. You're training your brain to default to your Sage powers instead of your saboteurs.

You're becoming mentally fit.

And mental fitness, your capacity to handle life's challenges with a positive mindset rather than getting upset and stressed, is the foundation for everything else you want to create in your life.

Your Invitation

I truly believe that mindfulness practice is not optional if you want to live fully and authentically. It's the training that makes all the other concepts in this book actually work in your real life, in real time, when it matters most.

So here's my invitation to you: Start today. Not tomorrow. Not when you have more time. Not when you feel ready.

Today.

Choose one small mindfulness practice, maybe just two minutes of mindful breathing when you wake up. Commit to it for one week. Just one week. Notice what changes. You could also choose to journal for five minutes before you start your day. Notice a difference.

I believe there are no coincidences, and there is a reason you're reading these words right now. Perhaps this is your moment. Your invitation to step off autopilot and into the present moment. Your opportunity to strengthen your mental fitness muscle and create the life you're meant to live.

Your Sage is waiting for you in the present moment.

Will you meet it there?

Reflection Questions

How much of your day do you spend truly present versus lost in thoughts about the past or future?

Which of the five components of mindfulness—attention, awareness, acceptance, non-identification, or choice—feels most challenging for you?

What are you avoiding feeling right now? What would happen if you allowed yourself to be present with that emotion?

Which of your saboteurs most often interrupts or undermines your attempts at mindfulness?

What would your life look like if you responded consciously to challenges instead of reacting automatically?

Start with just one question. Be present with it. Notice what emerges.

That's mindfulness in action.

Conclusion

MANIFESTING THE LIFE YOU CHOOSE

You've heard the saying, "Be careful what you wish for because you might just get it!"

This is the universal Law of Attraction at work, and it applies to all of us without question. But here's what I've learned through my years of coaching and my own journey: It's not just about wishing. It's about the thoughts you think, the perspective you choose, and the mental fitness you develop every single day.

Remember Diane? The talented artist who spent decades hiding her gift, convinced she wasn't worthy of recognition? Her external reality—the isolation, the odd jobs, the depression—perfectly mirrored what was going on inside her head. She saw herself as a victim. She judged herself as not good enough. She avoided opportunities because she believed she would fail.

And her life reflected all of it to her.

But here's what really happened when Diane transformed: She reconnected with her authentic self. That little girl who found comfort and joy in creating art, who painted because it made her soul sing, had been buried under decades of limiting beliefs and saboteur voices. The lies she was fed as a child about not being good enough, about her only value being in finding a husband, about art being just a hobby, those lies had silenced her inner child's true knowing.

When she learned to recognize her saboteurs, activate her Sage powers, and practice mindfulness daily, she didn't just change her behavior. She rediscovered who she truly was beneath all those layers of conditioning. She reconnected with her intuition, that quiet inner voice that had been trying to guide her all along, telling her she was meant to share her gift with the world.

That's what this book has been about: giving you the tools to consciously create the life you're meant to live by reconnecting with your authentic self, the self that existed before the world told you who you should be.

Early in this book, do you remember when we talked about your inner child and intuition? There was a reason we started there.

Your inner child holds the truth of who you are before the world got to you. Before your parents, teachers, society, and circumstances layered limiting beliefs onto your psyche. Before you learned to judge yourself, please others, avoid risk, and play small.

That child within you still knows what brings you joy. Still recognizes your authentic gifts. Still feels the pull toward your true purpose.

And your intuition? That's the voice of your Sage trying to guide you home to yourself.

But here's what happens: Your saboteurs drown out both of these essential voices. Your Judge tells you that your childhood dreams were naive and unrealistic. Your Hyper-Rational dismisses intuitive knowing as "just feelings" with no logical basis. Your Stickler insists you follow the rules and the prescribed path rather than listening to that quiet inner knowing. Your Victim convinces you that it's too late, that you've gone too far down the wrong road to turn back now.

And so you lose touch with the very parts of yourself that hold the map to your authentic life.

Diane's inner child knew she was an artist. Her intuition kept pulling her toward beauty, toward creation, toward sharing her vision with others. But her saboteurs, born from her father's dismissal of her worth, from society's narrow definition of a woman's role, from decades of reinforcing limiting beliefs, silenced those voices so completely that she almost forgot they existed.

The work we've done throughout this book isn't about becoming someone new. It's about remembering who you've always been. It's about clearing away the saboteur noise so you can finally hear your inner child's wisdom and your intuition's guidance.

When you practice mindfulness, you create a quiet space where these authentic voices can emerge. When you activate your Sage powers, especially Empathize and Explore, you reconnect with the wonder and openness of your inner child. When you intercept your saboteurs, you remove the barriers that have been blocking your intuitive knowing.

This is how you return to your authentic self. Not by adding more knowledge or trying harder or fixing what's broken. But by peeling away what was never truly you in the first place.

Unless we make a conscious effort to watch ourselves from the sidelines, our everyday thoughts and our reactions to the environment are largely habitual. We do our daily work, and we plan and we interact with our fellow human beings, but in between, we also have secret fears, grudges, and a great deal of negative self-talk.

How is your life going right now?

If you pay attention carefully, you'll begin to see that the reality outside yourself mirrors what is going on inside your head.

This isn't mystical thinking—it's neuroscience combined with the Law of Attraction. Your Judge Saboteur constantly criticizes you? You'll find yourself surrounded by criticism from others. Your Victim Saboteur tells you you're powerless? You'll keep attracting situations where you feel trapped. Your Avoider saboteur keeps you hiding? Opportunities will pass you by.

Your saboteurs don't just make you feel bad; they actively shape the reality you experience.

But here's the incredible truth: Your Sage powers work the same way. When you approach life with empathy, curiosity, creativity, clarity, and purposeful action, you attract people, circumstances, and opportunities that match that energy.

What you focus on expands.

If you are constantly worrying about this or that, then guess what? You will attract more events in your life to worry about. It is that simple.

Your Hyper-Vigilant saboteur scanning for everything that could go wrong? You'll find problems everywhere. Your Stickler saboteur is obsessing over imperfection? Nothing will ever be good enough. Your Restless saboteur jumping from one thing to the next? You'll never feel satisfied or complete.

And here's the tricky part: If you tell yourself NOT to worry about something, well, you are focused on it, so you ARE worried about it.

The trick is to think about what you DO want and not what you DON'T want.

This is where the Sage perspective becomes essential. Instead of focusing on what you're trying to avoid: failure, rejection, judgment, loss, you focus on what you're moving toward: growth, connection, creativity, purpose, and fulfillment.

Diane stopped focusing on hiding from criticism and started focusing on sharing beauty. That shift in focus changed everything.

What are you focusing on right now? Your limitations or your possibilities? Your fears or your gifts? Your saboteurs or your Sage?

Did I say it was easy? No, it's not easy to change a lifetime of habitual thinking, but just being aware of it is a step in the right direction.

This is where your daily mindfulness practice becomes non-negotiable. You will now begin to catch yourself in your internal dramas. You'll notice when your Judge is attacking you. You'll recognize when your Victim is taking over. You'll see the fork in the road appearing repeatedly throughout your day.

When you do catch yourself, try to change the thought to something that makes you feel better. If you feel better, you become 'unstuck' from your current drama and move on. Your perspective changes, and you are in the flow for the time being.

Sometimes, feeling better means that you will run through emotions such as anger or revenge first, but if it lifts you out of depression or despair, then it is a step in the right direction. This is moving up through the core energy levels we discussed earlier. You can continue to move up the emotional scale from there until you are feeling more positive emotions, such as pleasure, love, and gratitude.

This is the work. Not once, but again and again. Daily practice. Moment by moment. Choice by choice.

Remember: "If you keep doing what you've always done, you'll keep getting what you've always got."

You must change those habitual thoughts, self-talk, and reactions to get better results. You must strengthen your mental fitness muscle. You must practice intercepting your saboteurs and choosing your Sage perspective. You must commit to mindfulness as a daily practice, not an occasional retreat.

Consciously slowing down your mind and just being present, not focusing on the past or the future, will make a huge difference in your state of mind and your overall mood.

This is what we've been building toward throughout this entire book:

The ability to pause. To create space between stimulus and response. To stand at the fork in the road and consciously choose which path to take.

The awareness to recognize your saboteurs. To see them for what they are—old survival patterns that no longer serve you—rather than accepting their lies as truth.

The courage to feel your emotions fully. To practice acceptance, non-identification, and choice. To experience anger or fear or sadness without becoming them or being controlled by them.

The wisdom to apply the Three Gifts Technique. To find the knowledge, power, and inspiration hidden in every challenge. To turn obstacles into opportunities.

The commitment to activate your five Sage powers. To approach life with empathy, curiosity, creativity, clarity, and purposeful action.

Meditation, prayer, nature walks, or making a list of things you are grateful for are some ways to practice this presence. Practicing this a little every day will work wonders, I promise you!

I've seen it work wonders in my own life. I've witnessed it transform clients like Diane from disillusioned to purposeful, from hiding to shining, from victim to creator.

Just a final note here, because I want you to be prepared: As you are all aware, personal changes can sometimes bring about a certain amount of upheaval in your life, but that is perfectly normal.

When Diane started showing her artwork, she felt vulnerable and exposed. Some people weren't interested. Some conversations were awkward. Her old friendships shifted as she became more confident and less dependent. She had to navigate the discomfort of being visible after decades of hiding.

Growth isn't always comfortable. Change can be messy. As you practice these concepts and strengthen your mental fitness, things might feel chaotic for a while.

Your saboteurs will fight back, trying to pull you into familiar patterns. Relationships might shift as you set better boundaries and show up more authentically. Old coping mechanisms won't work anymore, and new ones will take time to develop.

Recognizing the chaos as part of the process will help to keep you moving forward.

This is where your Sage power of Navigation becomes essential. You're not lost, you're finding your way. You're not failing, you're learning. You're not broken, you're breaking free.

The chaos means you're changing. And change, even positive change, can feel uncomfortable before it feels natural.

Trust the process. Keep practicing. Stay present.

It is definitely possible to go from a disillusioned life to a life of purpose.

I know because I've lived it. I've guided countless women through this transformation. And I've watched them step into versions of themselves they once thought impossible.

You are not stuck with the life you have. You are not limited by your past. You are not defined by your saboteurs.

You have within you everything you need to create the life you're meant to live:

The question isn't whether you can transform your life. The question is: Will you?

Will you commit to the daily practice of mental fitness? Will you catch yourself in saboteur mode and choose differently? Will you pause at the fork in the road and take the Sage path? Will you stay present with uncomfortable emotions instead of running from them? Will you focus on what you want to create instead of what you want to avoid?

Will you listen to your inner child's wisdom and your intuition's guidance? Will you trust that quiet voice within you that has been trying to lead you home to yourself all along?

Will you show up, day after day, for the practice that changes everything?

Right now, in this moment, you're standing at a fork in the road.

Down one path, you can close this book and return to habitual patterns. Your saboteurs will be there, familiar and comfortable, offering you all the same thoughts and reactions you've always had. And you'll keep getting what you've always got.

Down the other path, your Sage is waiting. It's inviting you to something different. Something more. Something true.

The life you're meant to live isn't somewhere in the distant future, waiting for perfect conditions. It's here, now, in this present moment. It exists in every choice you make, every thought you think, every action you take.

You don't have to have it all figured out. You don't have to be perfect. You don't have to do this alone.

You just have to start. Today. Right now.

Choose one practice from this book, just one, and commit to it for one week. Maybe it's two minutes of mindful breathing each morning. Maybe it's catching yourself when your Judge saboteur attacks and choosing empathy instead. Maybe it's asking the Three Gifts questions when something challenging happens. Maybe it's journaling to reconnect with your inner child. Maybe it's pausing to listen to your intuition's guidance before making a decision. Maybe it's taking one immediate action toward a dream you've been avoiding.

One practice. One week. See what happens.

I believe there are no chance meetings, no coincidences, and there is a reason for everything. I truly believe that you were meant to read this book, at this time, for the lessons it can teach you and the transformation it can support.

Your Sage has been trying to reach you all along. Through every challenge, every setback, every moment of doubt, it's been there, waiting patiently, knowing what you're capable of. Your inner child has been waiting too, hoping you'd remember the dreams you once held, the joy you once knew, the authentic self you were always meant to be. And your intuition has been whispering guidance, even when the saboteur voices were so loud you couldn't hear it.

Maybe it's time to listen.

The life you choose is waiting to be manifested. Not through wishing, but through conscious daily practice. Not through perfection, but through presence. Not someday, but starting right now.

Your mental fitness journey begins with a single choice.

What will you choose?

A Personal Note

As a transformational life coach and mental fitness trainer, my mission is to encourage women to choose self-growth over the status quo, to reconnect with what is most important in their lives, and to lead their lives following their authentic purpose.

If Diane's story resonated with you, if you see yourself hiding a gift, stuck in saboteur patterns, longing for change but unsure how to begin, I want you to know that transformation is possible. Not just possible, but probable, when you commit to the daily practice of mental fitness.

You don't have to figure this out alone. As a coach, I partner with women to help them find the answers within themselves. We don't delve into the past to heal old wounds—we look at the here and now and how to move forward to a bright future.

If you're interested in seeing if we might be a good fit to work together, to get from where you are to where you want to be, I would be honored to explore that possibility with you.

But whether we work together or not, I hope this book has given you the tools, perspective, and inspiration to begin manifesting the life you choose.

Your Sage is waiting.

The present moment is here.

Your life of purpose is possible.

Will you take the first step?

With deep belief in your potential,

Juli

Acknowledgements

To Hanna Olivas, Catherine Cruz, Katrina Senne, and all the staff at She Rises Studios: Thank you for making this book possible. Your work and support are gratefully appreciated.

To All My Family and Friends: Thanks for all your support during this journey.

All my love,
Juli

About the Author

Julia Miezejeski is a certified professional coach. She was certified by the Institute for Professional Excellence in Coaching(IPEC). Life Coaching With Juli, her coaching practice, specializes in coaching high-achieving women who want to reconnect with their true purpose so they can create a legacy of meaningful impact without sacrificing their current success or compromising their authentic selves. Julia received her MBA from Pace University in New York and spent almost 30 years as a corporate executive and independent consultant. Her mission is to encourage women to choose self-growth over the status quo, to find/grow into their authentic purpose. She encourages women to live their lives according to their terms, even if they discover that means they have to make a 360-degree turnaround in their lifestyle. When Juli left her corporate career, she had to overcome many internal and external obstacles to achieve happiness as an entrepreneur. Her mission is to empower others to achieve their best life, no matter which path they choose.

LIFE COACHING WITH JULI

As a transformational life coach and mental fitness trainer, I partner with high-achieving women to reconnect with their deepest purpose so they can create a legacy of meaningful impact without sacrificing their current success or compromising their authentic selves.

Hi! My name is Juli Miezejeski.

My Journey to Transformational Life Coaching

The path that led me to become a transformational life coach wasn't a straight line – and that's exactly what makes my approach unique and effective. With an MBA in marketing and management science, I spent almost thirty years navigating the corporate world as a mid-level executive in high-tech, consulting, and publishing companies. On paper, I had achieved the traditional markers of success, but something was missing.

Throughout my corporate career, I maintained a deep fascination with psychology and human potential. This interest, while unfulfilled at the time, was quietly guiding me toward my true calling. The pivotal moment came when I met an executive coach who opened my eyes to a different way of creating impact in the world. This encounter sparked a profound realization: I could combine my extensive business experience with my passion for human development to help others navigate their own transformational journeys.

Upon pursuing my certification as a Professional Coach through The Institute for Professional Excellence in Coaching (iPEC), I made two life-changing decisions: to never return to the corporate environment and to dedicate myself to supporting high-achieving women who, like my younger self, are seeking deeper meaning and purpose in their lives.

Today, as a Certified Professional Coach and mental fitness trainer (currently pursuing certification as a Positive Intelligence Coach), I partner with women who are ready to move beyond conventional success to discover their authentic calling. My approach combines professional expertise with deep empathy – because I've walked the path from external achievement to internal fulfillment.

What sets my coaching apart is the unique blend of corporate understanding, professional coaching techniques, and personal transformation experience. I don't just teach or mentor; I partner with my clients on their journey, using both intuitive insight and proven methods to help them overcome obstacles and reconnect with what truly matters to them.

My mission is clear: to guide high-achieving women toward lives of purpose and fulfillment, helping them create the meaningful impact they're meant to make in the world. Whether you're feeling stuck in your success, searching for deeper meaning, or ready to discover your true calling, I'm here to partner with you on that transformational journey.

For complete information on all my services: Visit https://www.lifecoachingwithjuli.com

Bibliography

Access Karuna. (2023, February 16). *Is Inner Child Work Evidence-Based?* https://www.accesskaruna.org/blog/innerchildworkevidencebased

Assagioli, R. (2003, December 3). *Psychosynthesis*. In Wikipedia. https://en.wikipedia.org/wiki/Psychosynthesis

Bradshaw, J. (2018). *Homecoming: Reclaiming and Healing Your Inner Child*. John Bradshaw. https://www.johnbradshaw.com/books/homecoming-reclaiming-and-healing-your-inner-child

Bradshaw, J. (2024). *Homecoming: Reclaiming and Healing Your Inner Child*. Bantam

Carstensen, L. L. (2021). Socioemotional selectivity theory: The role of perceived endings in human motivation. *The Gerontologist*, 61(8), 1188-1196. https://doi.org/10.1093/geront/gnab116

Carstensen, L. L., Isaacowitz, D. M., & Charles, S. T. (1999). Taking time seriously: A theory of socioemotional selectivity. *American Psychologist*, 54(3), 165-181.

Charles, S. T., & Carstensen, L. L. (2003). Socioemotional selectivity theory and the regulation of emotion in the second half of life. *Motivation and Emotion*, 27(2), 103-123.

Dennis, M., Spiegler, B., Juranek, J., Bigler, E., Snead, O., & Fletcher, J. (2013). Neuroplasticity. In *StatPearls*. StatPearls Publishing. https://www.ncbi.nlm.nih.gov/books/NBK557811/

Edalat, A., Nazemi, M., & Razzaghi, T. (2022). Effectiveness of reparenting-based intervention using the self-attachment technique. *Journal of Clinical Psychology*, 78(4), 642-655.

Firman, J., & Russell, A. (2017). *What is Psychosynthesis?* [PDF]. Turning Point. https://www.turningpoint.ie/wp-content/uploads/2017/03/What-is-Psychosynthesis-Firman-and-Russell.pdf

Harvard Center on the Developing Child. (2025). Brain architecture: An ongoing process that begins before birth. https://developingchild.harvard.edu/key-concept/brain-architecture/

Hodgdon, H. B., Anderson, F. G., Heaphy, E. L., & Timm, T. M. (2021). A pilot study of IFS-informed individual psychotherapy with adult trauma survivors. *Journal of Trauma & Dissociation*, 22(4), 431-449.

Integrative Psychotherapy. (2023, November 11). *What Is An Inner Child | And What Does It Know?* https://integrativepsych.co/new-blog/what-is-an-inner-child

Koen, J. D., Hauck, N., & Rugg, M. D. (2019). The relationship between age, neural differentiation, and memory performance. *Journal of Neuroscience*, 39(1), 149-162. https://doi.org/10.1523/JNEUROSCI.1498-18.2018

Kohut, H. (1984). *How Does Analysis Cure?* University of Chicago Press.

Kolb, B., & Gibb, R. (2011). Brain plasticity and behaviour in the developing brain. *Journal of the Canadian Academy of Child and*

Adolescent Psychiatry, 20(4), 265-276. https://pmc.ncbi.nlm.nih.gov/articles/PMC3222570/

Park, D. C., Polk, T. A., Park, R., Minear, M., Savage, A., & Smith, M. R. (2004). Aging reduces neural specialization in the ventral visual cortex. *Proceedings of the National Academy of Sciences*, 101(35), 13091-13095.

Rugg, M. D., & Koen, J. D. (2019). Neural dedifferentiation in the aging brain. *Trends in Cognitive Sciences*, 23(7), 547-559. https://doi.org/10.1016/j.tics.2019.04.012

Sjöblom, A., Hedberg, P., Hommel, A., & Öhlen, J. (2016). Health throughout the lifespan: The phenomenon of the inner child reflected in events during childhood experienced by older persons. *International Journal of Qualitative Studies on Health and Well-being*, 11(1), 31486. https://pmc.ncbi.nlm.nih.gov/articles/PMC4912602/

Stein, M. (2019). Individuation. In *International Association of Analytical Psychology - Short Articles on Analytical Psychology*. https://iaap.org/jung-analytical-psychology/short-articles-on-analytical-psychology/individuation-2/

Teicher, M. H., Ohashi, K., & Khan, A. (2022). Developmental trauma: Conceptual framework, associated risks and comorbidities, and evaluation and treatment. *Frontiers in Psychiatry*, 13, 994276. https://pmc.ncbi.nlm.nih.gov/articles/PMC9352895/

Wikipedia contributors. (2004, November 15). *Inner child*. In Wikipedia. https://en.wikipedia.org/wiki/Inner_child

Additional Supporting References:

Capacchione, L. (1991). *Recovery of your inner child*. Simon & Schuster.

Jung, C. G. (1916/1928). The transcendent function. In *The Collected Works of C.G. Jung* (Vol. 8). Princeton University Press.

Jung, C. G. (1963). *Memories, dreams, reflections*. Vintage Books.

Li, S. C., Lindenberger, U., & Sikström, S. (2001). Aging cognition: From neuromodulation to representation. *Trends in Cognitive Sciences*, 5(11), 479-486.

Pfeiffer, E. (1977). Psychopathology and social pathology. In J. E. Birren & K. W. Schaie (Eds.), *Handbook of the psychology of aging* (pp. 650-671). Van Nostrand Reinhold.

Made in the USA
Coppell, TX
28 January 2026

70319816R00105